Advance Praise for *T*

M000221552

"Yes, there are hard-won lessons to be wrung from Cristina Nehring's ongoing odyssey as the single mother of a Down syndrome child and spun into lyric wisdom. But *The Child Who Never Spoke: 23 ½ Lessons in Fragility* is more than a guidebook to the uses and unexpected gifts of adversity. It is a love story, an adventure tale, an impetuous travelog, and a suspenseful medical saga (you can almost hear the hospital beeps in the background, the shuffle of footsteps down the halls) borne along by Nehring's buoyant breadth of spirit and the unbreakable bond with her daughter Eurydice. And the writing! So elegant and intimate. It's like hearing from a cherished friend after way too long."
—James Wolcott, author of the memoir *Lucking Out* and the essay collection *Critical Mass*

"Cristina Nehring is an extraordinary writer and this memoir tells an extraordinary story—vividly and bewitchingly. We all live among families with special needs children, but we have never read anything as intimate, revealing and celebratory about them as this page-turner of a book."
—Helen Epstein, author of *Children of the Holocaust* and *Getting Through It: A Year of Cancer During Covid*

"The narrator of Cristina Nehring's *The Child Who Never Spoke: 23 ½ Lessons in Fragility* is a woman determined to live on her own terms—free to pursue intellectual, creative and erotic adventure, until the unexpected intervenes: an unplanned daughter with exceptional needs. Over the course of twenty-three (and a half) short, heart-punching chapters, Nehring delivers to the reader the delight of getting to know her darling, exuberant daughter, and a serious meditation on what makes life most meaningful."
—Brian Morton, author of *Starting Out in the Evening* and *Tasha*

"...Cristina Nehring trades her life as a "romantic, a nomad, a solitary" for the ultimate act of partnership: motherhood. Though her dive into domestic life is full of seemingly cruel plot twists, Nehring draws from mothering a series of insights so tender they take the reader's breath away. By gently reframing the impositions and indignities of raising a 'special needs' child into the daily gift of living with 'Dice,' Nehring reveals a girl alive with joy and unadulterated love, who will leap into readers' hearts as indelibly as she leapt into her mother's."
—Heather Harpham, author of *Happiness: The Crooked Little Road to Semi-Ever After*

"If by reading a book you could become a slightly better human being, then this one might do it. At least it will remind you of what a wondrous adventure being a human can be. And how much that will depend on your ability and courage to embrace the challenges that inevitably come with it. Cristina Nehring has written a beautiful, moving, and I dare say edifying, tale of what her relentless embracing of Eurydice, "a unique, resplendent, radiant, irreplicable, individual human being", has brought not only to her, but to anyone reading this gem of a book."
—Goran Rosenberg, author of *A Brief Stop on the Road to Auschwitz*

"Journalist, scholar, romantic, Cristina Nehring found her life taking an unexpected turn when, in her mid-30s, she gave birth to a child with severe Down syndrome. Nehring's startling and poetic memoir of the first eight years of Eurydice's life is a compelling story--filled with anguish, laughter, adventures in and out of hospitals, and unvarnished observations about the joys and pains of unconditional love. Those who seek to know what makes us human should read and ponder this beautiful book."
—Daphne Patai, author of *What Price Utopia? Essays on Ideological Policing, Feminism and Academic Affairs*

"We try to control things. We can't. And how we respond to that conundrum depends on how much we're willing to learn. In *The Child Who Never Spoke*, Cristina Nehring tells us what happened when she, a nomadic romantic with a "robust contempt" for the very notion of parenting, got thrown a curveball as big as an asteroid: an accidental pregnancy and a daughter with Down syndrome. Hers is a story about losing freedom and gaining wisdom, yes, but what's miraculous is that Nehring presents that saga (with prose that glows like a Parisian summer night) as a romp: in spite of the serious struggles that she and Eurydice have faced along the way, the book is a veritable banquet of verve, a tale of two big-hearted survivors who surrender to the currents of love."
—Jeff Gordinier, author of *Hungry and X Saves the World*

"There is so much danger and love packed into this slender memoir. It's like reading Bukowski or Hunter S. Thompson. But it's a woman living them, with a small child, and so much more at stake. I was always worried for her and rooting for her and in the end incredibly inspired by her. In every dark place she finds love."
—Hanna Rosin, author of *The End of Men* and podcast director at *New York Magazine*

"Not for the faint of heart—a true adventurer accomplishes amazing feats and encounters truly harrowing situations. Nehring turns her heart inside out with her prodigious love for her daughter."
—Sandra McElwee, author of *Who's the Slow Learner? A Chronicle of Inclusion and Exclusion* and mother of Sean McElwee, Down Syndrome star of the TV series *Born This Way*.

"This memoir takes you on a ride of "Oh yes, that's me" and "That is also me" and then drags you into both heaven and undertow combined. A free-spirited bohemian travel writer who never wanted children is suddenly presented with an emotional and intellectual challenge, a baby, her baby, a baby with special needs. And, together they wrap themselves around the universe, through thick and thin in a backwards Candide duet celebration tale where behind every window is a new starry night garden, where all is for the best and this *is* the best of all possible worlds.

—Millicent Borges Accardi, author of *Quarantine Highway* and National Endowment of the Arts Poetry Fellow

The Child Who Never Spoke

The Child Who Never Spoke

23½ Lessons in Fragility

Cristina Nehring

Heliotrope Books
New York

I'd like to dedicate this book to
Eurydice Rafaella Tess,
my girl and my guru,
with love

Also by Cristina Nehring:

*A Vindication of Love: Reclaiming Romance
for the 21st Century*

Journey to the Edge of the Light

L'Amour a L'Américaine

23-et-Demi

Contents

There is a crack, a crack in everything
That's how the light gets in.

—Leonard Cohen

Introduction

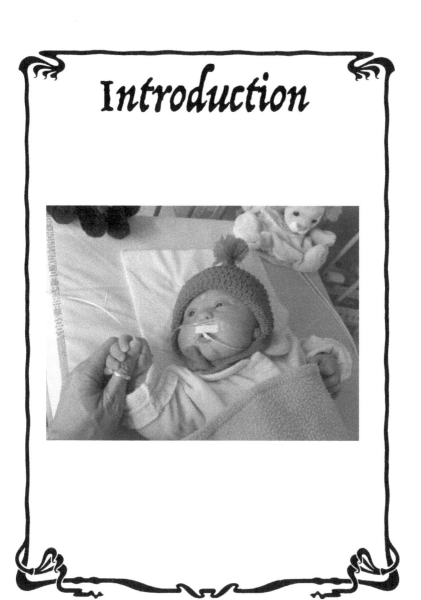

Two-day old Eurydice in the ICU
of Trosseau Hospital

If there is a woman in the world who should not have had a special child, it is me. I didn't want *any* child. I've never wanted a child. It's the single subject on which I've been consistent my whole life. Since I was four years old and people gave me plastic baby dolls, I declared: "I don't want a baby." I declared it like a metronome. I declared it at four, fourteen, twenty-four, and thirty-four. No biological clock kicked in for me. Or rather: it may have kicked and ticked, but I couldn't have cared less.

My life was that of a nomad, an adventurer, a romantic, a solitary, driven, night-owling writer. I had a robust contempt for people who "passed the baton" to the next generation. Having children is what you do when you give up on your own life, I believed. It is when you stop thinking you may *become* a writer-explorer-actor-genius, that you decide to *give birth to* a writer-explorer-actor-genius. Becoming pregnant is an act of resignation. And just in case there's a wee bit of hope for yourself remaining by the time you give birth, the next few years knock it out of you for good and real.

Where once you could write all night—drinking red wine and white spirits to keep the words rushing; where once you could pick up and travel around the globe at a moment's notice, staying in fleabag hotels, hitchhiking with strangers and occasionally sleeping with them, now you had to lead a regulated, routinized, forward-planning and safety-checked life. A life in which you expend most of your waking energy attending to an excretory system not your own, a digestive and urinary and respiratory system not your own, a pattern of naps and nose-blowings, meals and mindless walks in the park.

Where once, perhaps, you sang your heart out to glean a standing ovation from crowds of distinguished critics, now you sing your heart out—often at greater length and with more stress—to obtain the dropping of an irritated infant's eyelids. "Oh how fallen, how changed!" as one of Milton's angels says when he sees Lucifer, still recently the star of heaven, descended onto earth and turned into a homely devil. "Oh how fallen, how changed," said I when I saw friends of mine—once sexy, glamorous, and full of promise—now with spittup clinging to their thickening shoulders. What a waste of genius and beauty, thought I.

Lest there be any doubt: I got pregnant by accident. I got pregnant with a beautiful young Greek man who also happened to be fiery and proud, as well as impossible and underemployed. One might say I was on the rebound from a relationship with his polar opposite: a man some years my senior (25), where Vasilis was some years my junior (4). My ex-fiancé is an intellectual, a workaholic, a controversial author. Vasilis is a waiter.

He is also a man with the distinction of not having

one book in his house. And yet he is unintimidated by Oxford professors, well-known novelists, or powerful politicians—with a surprising number of whom he seems to have had love affairs. When I smuggled him onto stage to attend a speech by Greece's candidate for president, son of its late president, Andreas Papandreou, he impressed me by answering the guards' question about his identity by gesturing with consummate confidence at his lettered T-shirt: "I am a waiter at *Tamam*," said he, tilting toward the small taverna he worked. Not a journalist, an interpreter, a party member, a friend of the Papandreou clan (all of which I'd urged him to imply), not a movie star (with his looks he could have passed as anything he wanted), not even "in the tourist industry," but *a waiter*. At *Tamam*. And in case there was any doubt remaining: he pointed to his T-shirt.

It was then that I fell in love with him. It was then that I fell in love in my head, that is—for I'd already fallen in love in my heart some weeks earlier. This although he was the first and only man I'd ever slept with whose name I did not remember in the morning. We had met in the alleys of Chania—the picturesque western seaport of Crete— where he was born and I'd come to write a travel article and stayed to finish a book. Fireworks had gone off on both sides; we'd talked until four in the morning on my rented patio in the company of my landlord, and then the landlord had gone to bed, and we, we had tumbled into each other's arms. When I woke up in the morning I did not remember if it was Michalis or Dimitrius or Vasilis or Panagiottis. I looked at the high cheekboned youth on the pillow beside me, the shock of wild, dark hair. "*Agapi mu*," I said gingerly: "My love."

I learned his name later that day when I met him—as I always did for the next few months—in his restaurant on a winding cobblestone street. He had no phone number then, and he has no phone number now. The way to speak to him was always the same: track him down in the flesh. So I came running to him barefoot from the patio where I labored to write in the morning. Crete is warm, and so are the cobblestones. I had never had a problem with getting my feet dirty. They had been the color of soot since I arrived.

So I ran to him on black feet and stalled to see if he would let me kiss him on the street. Greek men usually disown their girlfriends (and indeed their wives) in public. But Vasilis beamed at me, so I planted a kiss on his lips in full view of the unruly lunch guests, the elbowing tourists, and the crooked Cretan grandfathers with their tiny coffee cups. Thus began the collision course that was our love.

One year later I was pregnant. I was also convinced that our relationship would not work. Indeed, it had been this realization that had ironically "saved" us a month earlier— that had breathed joy back into our companionship at a time we had been struggling unhappily to make our lives mesh. After weeks of miserable and dramatic scenes—Vasilis smashing the door to my rental apartment, spying on me from rooftops, furiously prancing around in a skirt of mine to show me it was see-through—we had resolved to break up. We had decided we were not right for each other; we had mutually given up on the business of making a life together. And almost immediately our passion reignited.

With the pressure removed, the expectations halted, and the date of my departure from Crete fast approaching, we plummeted into a lyrical nostalgia for what might have been, what was, what could perhaps be if we were not prisoners of our cultures, our temperaments, our vastly divergent educations. It was the tenderest time of our relationship. We took long walks, climbed into the ruins of abandoned houses, and lounged there together under a tangle of grapevines and jasmine. Our hearts filled with posthumous love.

And then there came that feeling in my gut. A tickle. A lump. I jumped into the blue Cretan sea and noticed I could not flatten my abdomen as I could before. I told Vasilis. He had always said he wanted a child with me. But he did not react well. "I will never change my base," were the first words from his mouth. As though I had become pregnant to suggest he follow me to my home in California. Or Paris, the city where I'd lived for ten years. Or indeed a single kilometer from the suburb of Chania where he presently rented. Next to a chicken coop. He was committed to his way of living, as he was committed to no woman or man.

I decided to get an abortion. I was on my way out of a relationship. I was penniless. A free-lance writer has by definition no salary, only sporadic (and usually slender and tardy) paychecks when she manages to propose, negotiate, research, execute, edit, and see through to publication an article or book. It had taken me several years to come close to completing a book. I had no health plan, no insurance, no family money, no safety net. Most importantly, of course, I had little or no interest in becoming a parent.

This interest diminished—to the extent such was possible—when Vasilis and I saw a Cretan gynecologist who informed us that one was expected to breastfeed an infant six times a day. Somehow I had gotten the sense it was perhaps once a day. Mind you, I'd never looked into the matter, but I simply could not imagine anyone would reproduce if they understood they had to strip off their sweater, hunker down in some hidden cubby hole, and place their progeny on their bare bosom for forty-five minutes half a dozen times every day for one year. Since then, I've realized it's almost always more frequent than that—at least for a few months. But even the conservative Greek estimate was enough to send me into a tailspin. "My mood is extremely bad," announced Vasilis, ever anticipating my injuries and appropriating them.

He was not a man to rely on. Not for the raising of spirits and not for the provision of support, moral or material. As my pregnancy progressed—from four weeks to six to eight, it was he who became temperamental, explosive, had cravings, mood swings, and black depressions. My own pregnancy proceeded swimmingly. I ignored all the advice. I drank; I carried extraordinarily heavy suitcases; I biked over curbs and cobblestone, hills and dales; I flew in military airplanes to report on French President Nicolas Sarkozy; I stayed up until the wee hours of the morning. The only tip I took was from a designer friend in Los Angeles: "*Don't read pregnancy advice*," she said. "It will only drive you mad."

And, what, after all, was the worst that could happen to me? That I'd miscarry? Nobody could frighten me with that prospect. It was the opposite prospect that scared me—having a successful delivery. And yet even that was entering the realm of the imaginable. At a certain moment in my third month, I decided to return to the United States and consider this pregnancy apart from Vasilis. I yearned to consult with my old friends, with my ex-fiancé. I knew some of my girlfriends had tried impossibly hard to get pregnant. I'd not tried at all. Perhaps I should play the hand the jocular Greek gods had dealt me? If my nearest and dearest encouraged me, perhaps I would.

They discouraged me. Across the board. "I hate to say this, Cristina, but I don't think there's any way you can have this child," said one of my favorite persons, himself father to a beautiful teenager: "The context's just too impossible."

"Make your own decision," said my ex, Russell, who I'd never ceased to love, "but if you have this child, there's no future for us."

"*Don't worry*," said a psychologist he'd taken me to see in past years: "If you have an abortion, I'll be there for you. And so will Russell. It will take a lot of therapy sessions to get over it. It will take a lot of work. But I'm right here waiting to help."

Perhaps it was partly rebellion that made me keep the child. To hell with it, I thought: if I am going to have to work a lot to *not* have a child I might as well work a lot to have one. The six breast feedings a day suddenly no longer seemed that daunting. They seemed almost tempting compared to the sixty sessions of therapy I was presumably facing if I aborted. If I was going to work like hell to get over a death, I might as well work like hell to make a life. Or so I finally thought. Fuzzily. Indignantly. Childishly. Churlishly. Feistily. Fragilely.

A few months later I flew alone to Paris, my adopted hometown, and the only place I knew I could give birth for free. I had burnt bridges with everybody who was important to me. Vasilis was no longer speaking to me.

Never one to use the telephone, he had cut off also mail and e-mail communication. My ex-fiancé was my best friend, but he deeply disapproved of my decision. On the airplane, I realized once more how bizarre this decision really was.

Eight months pregnant, I was assigned bulkhead seating. This means extra legroom; it also means you're in the infant row. It was as though I'd been placed there to demonstrate just how phenomenal an idiocy I was committing. To my left and right, for the next fourteen hours, were squalling, dribbling, accusatory-looking babies. "It is amazing," I scribbled in my journal that day, "how remote these little bald-gazed creatures still are to me, how shocking their cries."

…

It was 9:14 pm, and Eurydice's bald cry took its place among the elements. She had started to stir at 9 am that morning, a Monday morning, like a good French citizen going to work after a weekend. *"Travailler plus pour gagner plus!"* was the slogan of President Sarkozy. "Work more to earn more!" Get up early; get out early; get home early. The French citizen in my womb had heeded her president's call. She got up early. She was out early. But she was not, as it happens, to go home early.

For the next twelve and a half days, Eurydice Rafaella was in the Intensive Care Unit at the hospital in which I gave birth to her, which happened, by a fluke, to be the best known children's hospital in France. And a happy fluke it was. For Eurydice had only been three hours at my side when a nurse came to our hospital room to take her away since she was not getting enough oxygen. To this moment I am not sure if this was a lie. She seemed to me to be doing well that night, though she certainly needed oxygen in the following days. But the doctor, the nurses, the midwife—everybody, it turns out, in the delivery room but me—had noticed signs of Down syndrome.

What I *had* noticed is that the child whom I had given a very romantic name did not look very romantic. Where I had imagined a long-limbed, willowy creature with sharply defined facial features and perhaps even the obvious sensitivity of her father, Eurydice had short limbs and a perfectly round moon face. She reminded me of a Buddha—or a stodgy classical philosopher. Maybe I should call her Seneca instead of Eurydice, I thought fleetingly.

Then again I did not know how children were supposed to look at birth. I had reason to hope they all looked like Seneca. "Do you...do you think she's cute?" I asked the midwife hesitantly. I tried to make myself sound like a grateful mother fishing for compliments about her obviously adorable newborn.

"Sure," said the midwife, watching me closely. As I left the delivery room, she cleared her throat: "You simply *have to* hope for the best." She gripped my arm, eyes aflame.

The supervising doctor—a blonde Russian woman—told me later that she had gone home and wept. "I knew you were a writer," she said, "a person whose life is intellect. I felt terrible for you. I cried the entire night."

I'd not cried. Rather, with Eurydice whisked away, I'd puzzled over the clothes I'd bought for her, now stacked neatly in the hospital closet across from my bed. They were very feminine, very mermaidy. They seemed strangely misconceived for the little Buddha I had borne. I wondered how I would live with this Buddha for the next eighteen years.

Or the next fifty, as it happened. Only "a small minority of Down syndrome victims ever live independently," as I eventually heard. The majority—if they do not go to state institutions—live with their parents until death. That death, admittedly, is early. In 1929, it was at around age nine. In the 1970s, it was just over twenty. Now it's edging up toward fifty. A success but also a challenge. Dementia comes well before death. People with Down syndrome often show signs of Alzheimer's before forty, making them depend on their parents still more, even while they recognize them far less.

But all this I did not know yet. I knew only that I did not feel very motherly. My baby seemed an odd stranger—as odd as a pudgy bank manager I might run into in Manhattan. It all felt like an ill-construed blind date. A marriage arranged by an idiot. The only consolation I had was that, in my hard-headedness, I had been right all along: There was no such thing as maternal instinct. It was a myth made up by patriarchs eager for an excuse to incarcerate their wives in the nursery. I would prove it by breastfeeding Eurydice for six months, as instructed, and then turning her gradually and gently over to her big, child-loving Greek family on Crete.

For Vasilis had come to the birth in Paris, despite having gone incommunicado for half a year. He had ignored my proposal that we meet three months before Eurydice's estimated arrival date, but had turned up on my doorstep in Paris a few days before her delivery. All smiles and scintillating good looks, he had arrived expecting, like the Americans in Iraq, to be greeted with flowers and candy. His camera was raised; it was set to "video." The happy reunion was ready to roll.

Vasilis is a man spoiled by women. The youngest in his family, he was doted on by his sister, mother, cousins, aunts. Before long he was doted on by a sizeable part of the female population of Chania. Not only was his smile disarming, his torso rippling, and his locks cherubic, but his conversation was at once intimate and emphatically intelligent.

His intelligence was something I'd remembered when I'd defied my mentors and kept the pregnancy. He might be completely unambitious, but any child of ours would be brilliant. And beautiful. She would have every genetic advantage. As hard as the whole project seemed on the outside, on the inside—on the level of chromosomes—it was going to be easy. And spectacular.

Man plans. Gods laugh.

Vasilis arrived on my doorstep and sucked my tongue into his mouth. I turned away, spluttering. He held my face in his hands and tore off a pearl earring. I never found it again. Nor did I find my passion for him again. After months of making medical visits, remodeling my studio to accommodate a child, organizing endless bureaucratic matters relative to the birth, hauling clothes and carriages across the city, buying infant furniture—all while seven, eight, nine months pregnant and *alone*—I now saw Vasilis as a feckless and irresponsible adolescent. What attraction I'd once felt for him was dead.

He was not used to this. He punished me for it over

the next weeks by trading his passive negligence for active hostility. Only in the delivery room did he catch himself. Suddenly buoyant, he danced around in a light-blue paper medical coat and shot pictures of every detail, including— were it not for the midwife's protest—of the placenta. I have pictures of Eurydice's dark head emerging from my thighs. I have pictures of her thick umbilical cord and her first attempt to breastfeed. I have evidence that she looked, more or less incontrovertibly, like the Buddha.

…

I wonder, sometimes, whether the fates are shrewder than we think. If Eurydice had had an easier time of it at the beginning of her life, I do not know that I would have connected with her as fiercely and as violently as I did. For it was only after I trudged over to Intensive Care the day following the birth and found her in a little glass box, like Sleeping Beauty, with tubes going into her small nose and electrodes taped to her tiny chest and swaths of scotch tape disfiguring her alabaster face, that my heart leapt up. This was not the spoilt superkid I saw every day on the Boulevard Saint Germain. Nor was it the Buddha. This was a suffering innocent, the gentle child I had irresponsibly brought into the world and that was now hooked up to all the torture instruments of modern science on my account. I yearned to gather her up out of her glass box and press her to my chest and assure her that—*no matter what*—it would all be well, I would stand by her until the end of time, and I would fight for her so hard the world would reel off its axis if it stood in our way.

But strangely, Eurydice did not seem tortured. Perhaps after the crowded womb the hospital box felt spacious. The wires, the stickies all over her body, the doctors' instruments in her sheets—it was all just normal to her. Normalcy is what you know, and this was what Eurydice knew about life on earth. I gazed adoringly through the glass at my warrior-girl. At once Sleeping Beauty and Penthesilea, the Amazon queen. She had already, I mused, overcome more than I had. So much medical misery so early in life.

All the while I never doubted I would take her home by nightfall. A temporary oxygen problem related to birth trauma, the nurses had told me. But one day became two; two days became three; three days became four. They wanted to test her heart: sometimes the heart was the source of respiratory distress. And then came the call to the hospital room I was allowed to inhabit despite the fact that I was no sicker than any woman who had recently given birth. "The good news," said the doctor, "is her heart is fine. But we'd like to meet with you and the father. What time does he usually come see you?" I was too self-conscious, in that instant, about my ignorance of Vasilis' schedule to wonder why it was the doctor—who had thus far conferred only with me—wished to meet us together. Vasilis was free as a bird. He never told me when or if he'd come visit. I never asked. He turned up at some moment in the afternoon or evening, ate my tray of hospital food if it was still there (food in Paris was too expensive, he complained), and skipped down to see Eurydice. Soon he'd go out for a cigarette break. Usually he wouldn't return. Ditto the next day.

"I'll try to find out," I said.

Some hours later, Vasilis and I filed down to Intensive Care. The doctor came. Two doctors came. Three doctors. And then a fourth doctor. "Let's go to a different room," said the one in charge. We followed them down a long corridor, an awkward silence imposing itself. Our shoes shuffled loudly on the linoleum. Fabric rustled. We arrived in a dingy conference room, and sat around a large table, the doctors on one side, Vasilis and I on the other. I felt like I was about to be read my rights.

But no. They began—as I subsequently learned is standard operating procedure—by reiterating the good news: no heart troubles. Even the respiratory problems would pass. On the other hand, specialists had noticed characteristics which pointed to a genetic anomaly. I was in the dark. Vasilis was not. He who had stayed out of the conversation since his French was as slight as the doctors' English, suddenly leaned forward. "Down syndrome," he stated.

The doctors looked taken aback. "Yes," said Doctor Number One. "I mean," she tried to rewind, "that is the suspicion. That is the worst case scenario."

Eurydice had signs. The short neck. The round face. The almond-shaped eyes. An occasionally thrusting tongue. And yes, there was a telltale horizontal crease across the middle of her hand. A space between her first and second toe. And this potpourri of insignia was supposed to doom her to a lifetime of second-class-citizenship.

"She will always be the child on the street everyone turns to laugh at," sobbed the blonde Russian doctor to me later that day. She was not part of the official team in the conference room, and she'd not heard that the test results were still outstanding—nor that hers were not the words one tells new parents in a politically correct society. But her candor touched me. I was grateful for it. Even as I began to gird myself to resist its content.

Vasilis and I signed papers allowing the doctors to perform the desired tests, but we did not await the results. We knew the results. We were almost surprised to be summoned back into the conference room the following week. Had they discovered something else? Did she have cancer as well? We were relieved when the four doctors simply clasped their hands over and under each other and ceremoniously announced that Eurydice did indeed have Down syndrome. Their tests had confirmed as much.

"I know," I said. "Can we take her home now?" There followed speeches about genetics, accidents, the 21st chromosome splitting into three parts rather than two. This causing developmental delays and a bouquet of other possible health problems, including leukemia, heart illness, muscle weakness, premature aging, respiratory disorders, intestinal dysfunction, eye and ear troubles, and palate malformation.

"Now can I take her home?" I repeated.

My experiences with my daughter had been increasingly sweet. I went to the ICU several times a day to breastfeed her, but more importantly, I talked with her, and she huddled in the hollow of my neck and looked up into my face with eyes that were every day more inquisitive. Over the past nine days she had become the bright light among the dark prognoses, the dark moods, and the dark accusations that swirled around me. I fled to her from Vasilis's bitter looks and the Russian's black prognoses. She was the tragedy we were all gathered around to discuss and, at the same time, she was the escape from that tragedy. She hovered above her ailment like a flame hovers above wax, like a genie drifts above the bottle.

...

The day I came home from the hospital Eurydice stayed. We were supposed to leave together, but when the day and the hour struck, her blood oxygenation was still too low. Unhooked from her nasal infusion, the machines above her bed began to beep and blink. So I took the metro home alone one night at the end of April. It was raining. I had fed her all day, and kissed her around the tubes in her face, and labored to entertain her. Sometimes I ran out of things to say. Look at you, I observed to myself grimly: all your education does not suffice to stimulate a *mentally challenged infant*.

The truth is I had never talked to an infant before. All I knew is I disliked how people around me talked to children. The dripping falsehood, the affected surprise, the gooey, chewy, sugary voice, the deliberately mispronounced words. I hoped to talk to my girl soberly, as to a soulmate. Only it was dicey when the soulmate did not talk back. My imagination faltered. So did my spirit. Even my body was worn after ten days behind hospital doors.

The night I came home, I'd been kicked out of my room on the maternity ward at breakfast and hadn't eaten since the day before. Overnight bag in hand, I knocked on the door of the apartment Vasilis had inhabited alone since Eurydice's birth. No answer. I extracted my keys from my bag, unlocked, opened, and found the father of my child sprawled on my sofa, feet up on the backrest, playing computer games he'd installed on my laptop. The apartment was devastation. The air was saturated with smoke. I greeted him teasingly, and waited for him to get up. He kept on playing.

I set down my luggage and walked over to the

refrigerator. I was thirsty. Starving. The refrigerator was empty. I looked again. I had never seen it so empty before. Even the condiments were gone. It had been full when I left. Now there was not so much as a bottle of water.

I waited for Vasilis to go to the bathroom and stole my apartment keys from his backpack. The next day I left for the hospital and hoped he would lock himself out. I was too sickened to argue with the man who had once asked me to have his child. I simply wanted him gone.

He did not leave then. But he left a week later. He phoned me about the keys in the hospital; we had an outspoken conversation; I gave him another chance. He blew it, probably on purpose. I think he wanted to go. I don't know. But I asked him to leave again. He took a train to Germany the next afternoon and informed me he would now "play with the trains of Europe" for some months. He left no address, no telephone, no support. He left nothing, in fact, besides the smell of his tobacco.

Eurydice was home, by that time, and I had long mastered the art of fleeing to her soft arms from his stern anger. Now it was just the two of us. I, the die-hard romantic, author of a forthcoming book on love, was alone with an infant. A "special" infant. In a big city not my own. The infant and I were the new couple.

...

People with Down syndrome, as the doctors explained at the Intensive Care Unit, don't have *less* genetic material than the rest of us, they have more. Where average people have twenty-three chromosome pairs, persons with Down syndrome have an extra half pair.

In this extra half lies the source of the dark medical prognoses, altered learning patterns, and unusual physical features. In this accidental bonus lies the source of their shorter lives and—possibly—greater hearts.

Eurydice has twenty-three-and-one-half chromosome pairs and this book has twenty-three-and-one-half chapters—one for each life lesson I've been able to glean from her (if not always follow) since she was born.

Often these are lessons I stumbled past previously, that I've run across during my readings of favorite essayists or philosophers; that I've overlooked in my haste to become an indomitable career woman. But Eurydice wrote them in blood, not ink. She is a more credible teacher than any yogi, a more forgiving one than any Stoic, a more lovely one than Montaigne or Emerson or Simone de Beauvoir.

And her teaching? Over and over again it seems to do with fragility, with risk. Both of these we ordinarily read as undesirable; we associate them with darkness. But Eurydice shows us that it is when we appear weakest that we are, in fact, strongest, when our losses sting most, our celebration might be most vivid, when we appear most broken, we are, perhaps, most whole. "There is a crack in everything," sings Leonard Cohen, "that's where the light comes in." That and nowhere else: We are luster-less without our fissures, characterless without our losses, bloodless without our disappointments.

"The I is the sum of its defeats" says French novelist Michel Houellebecq. Our strength is built on these defeats. Our joy depends on the transmutation of pain, the exploitations of disadvantage. And when we put the most of ourselves on the line, we win the most.

It is a counterintuitive message, especially in a day that idolizes achievement and intelligence, high test scores and low risk. But perhaps it is a pertinent one. I want to lay it into your hands for assessment.

Chapter 1

Keep Moving

Eurydice, calmed, after hours of riding in her baby carriage

It hadn't been long that Eurydice and I were in our garret when she developed a show-stopping case of colic—infantile screaming for no medically transparent reason.

Destiny staggers its blows, I thought darkly as I slipped a bottle between her lips and tufts of cotton into my ears. It fools you into imagining you might, in fact, be able to handle a situation; then, once you are locked in, it ratchets up the heat. Had Eurydice exhibited this particular behavior as the bad news about her genes was rolling in at the maternity ward and her father was on his way out, God only knows what I'd have done. But this particular bomb did not strike until a month into the game—and by that time I was lost. I was in love and I was along for the ride.

So I hung on for dear life as my sweetly cooing daughter turned into a wolverine. "Rock her, rock her," hissed my child-savvy friends, and rock I did. But soon rocking would not suffice; only running would stay the storm. So I'd abandon dinner entrées and dinner companions, swathe Eurydice in blankets, pack her into her bright orange baby carriage and start to run. Up and down our sidewalk-less street we ran, dodging green trash trucks and spilling loaded trash bins, weaving in and out of traffic like a biker evading the law.

Within minutes the carriage no longer had its dulcifying effect; I padlocked it to a street lamp, disembarked its inhabitant and carried her through the nocturnal city in my arms. This was no easy feat for Eurydice was so floppy due to low muscle tone that her body would drape backwards over my arms like a party streamer. Bystanders flinched at the sight of us, and signaled to me that my child was not in an alive position. And yet Eurydice would be taking deep, long breaths and gazing about bright-eyed. That was my pay-off for running: Eurydice would recline in my arms with tender complicity, and I would begin to entertain her with ungenerous observations about the smugly seated coffee drinkers we passed.

There was one café in particular that we always traversed on our night-time excursions. I later grasped that it was a speed-dating venue. It was always packed with cocktail-nursing couples; in any case I always felt irritated navigating through its sidewalk spill-over with a spread-eagled babe in my arms.

"Look at that sot over there," I'd nudge Eurydice. "He just sat in his date's salsa. Bad move." I'd shake my head at Eurydice dubiously and she'd shake her own little head dubiously back.

She started giggling early. It may be the only milestone she reached ahead of developmental schedule, but the speed daters of *La Perle* can bear witness that a swaddled newborn laughed uproariously in their midst. Some spun around to confirm they were in fact being mocked by an infant, I shrugged apologetically and tossed a glance toward the milk bottle poking out of my shoulder bag. "Spiked," I said.

And we moved on, through good and bad neighborhoods, fashionable and fishy company. I often ended up near train stations. The *Gare de L'Est* and the *Gare du Nord* were only a few minutes apart and when I'd walked by them at night in the past I had always been uncomfortably aware of being taken for a prostitute. What other business would a woman in a short dress and blonde hair have exploring the hood at night?

And yet, I always took anxious care not to loiter, not to look in my purse, not to allow eye-contact or send any other signal that I might be waiting, open to an interaction. Now with a baby in my arms it was so much easier! I was no longer a call-girl in the eyes of the denizens, I was just plain lost. Predatory young men looked at me and looked away again with barely dissimulated disappointment. Others addressed a brotherly warning to me: "Do you know, Madame, that this is not a good area?" Did I need directions to a street or hotel?

What I usually needed were directions to the baby carriage. As often as not I couldn't recall where on our pilgrimage I'd shackled it. The trip home was always longer than the trip out, since a search operation would need to be inserted. If I was unlucky, Eurydice would fall asleep on the final stretch and wake precisely as I hauled her up the three flights to our flat—at which point the entire wrapping-descending-running operation would start again.

We must have done hundreds of kilometers this way in Eurydice's first months of life. I careened through corners of town I didn't know existed, strolled through exhibits I've entirely forgotten. When there was a perceptible lull in the baby carriage, I'd give the handbrake a sharp tug and drop to the ground earthquake style. If it was the hardwood floor under a Jackson Pollack in the Pompidou Museum that was fine; if it was the cobblestones next to a street bum, that was fine too—and I'd whip out my notepad. The trick was to use every instant of quiet before the soundtrack resumed. "Readiness is all," Shakespeare says somewhere in *Hamlet*. This became my mantra. When opportunities were so rare, I couldn't afford to be unready.

For what I feared most desperately in becoming a mother was ceasing to be a writer. More precisely: I feared ceasing to hear my own thoughts. It was not that I'd achieved such monumental successes with my published thoughts so far, but that didn't mean I didn't hope to do so.

My best literary output thus far had probably been in the realm of letter writing. Love letter writing. Nothing ever seemed to me as urgent; posterity and my publishers mattered far less than the man with whom I was currently infatuated. I had a hard time whipping up interest in abstract assignments or editors and university advisers— unless of course I fell in love with them which, mercifully, was quite often.

And yet my desire to make sense of the world in words—to slice through the yarn of cliché in which I saw my life and other lives so thickly enwrapped, to offer a flash of clarity, of consolation or inspiration at once to my readers as to myself—that desire was violent in me.

I often wished I could write to the world as I could write to a man into whose thrall I had fallen. To make love to the world in prose! To reveal everything. Give everything. Dare everything.

This hard-earned ecstatic communion with my reading public always lay to me somewhere in the distant but pre-destined future. And then came the "special birth," and the realization that my energies would need to be spent indefinitely and overwhelmingly on a child, a child unlikely to share my desire to discuss ideas. The future loomed dark and vacant ahead.

And yet. What I scribbled on my note pads between sprints down the street with Dice was different from what I'd scribbled before. It was sloppier but also wider, wilder, purer.

Perhaps bolting through town had a cleansing effect on my brain. All the impressions that rushed through me as I hurtled into new alleys and emergencies were having the effect of a river directed through a still pool. Suddenly all the hidden life at the bottom was being tossed up; the rocks cleared of sediment, the odors dispersed. Glinting objects were appearing every moment and being flushed to a shine. The noise was deafening and the glimpses momentary, but the sense of productive chaos, of renewal, was not to be mistaken.

"The scholar loses no hour that the man lives," says Ralph Waldo Emerson in my favorite of his essays, "Experience." We are forever afraid of losing time from our art, our profession, our vocation when we answer the summons of daily life, its exasperations and distractions its duties and sacrifices. And yet what we lose in hours we gain in powers. "The true scholar grudges every opportunity of action past as a loss of power. Action," he intones, "is pearls and rubies to his discourse."

Not that Emerson was well-placed to make this point; unlike his far less successful writer friend, Margaret Fuller, who threw herself into every revolution, embraced every social engagement, risked every heartbreak and died in a shipwreck, Emerson stood careful guard over his equanimity, sequestering himself for much of his life in a mansion presided over by his silently estranged wife.

For my part I'd come a long way since my life with my graduate school boyfriend who flicked on white noise machines when studying in order to cancel any stray sound. I'd come a long way from my years of being chained catatonically to a desk staring at computer screens in ambush of inspiration.

"The best ideas come to a man while walking," said Nietzsche: Any idea you hatched sitting on your backside is bloodless and suspect. Was there truth here? Could change of scenery, of perspective, situation or life be necessary to real thinking—indeed good coping? Did Emerson (who lived to seventy-nine) publish his last great essay volume at forty-one because he *had* become so sedentary? Do we have to keep scrambling to our feet and bolt into a new wood, a new clearing, a new catastrophe if we hope to think fresh thoughts and invent new solutions to our life questions?

"Aiiiiii!" came a cry from the orange vinyl at my side.

Not that my time between sprints through Paris was spent chiefly with fresh thoughts; the largest part was occupied with French paperwork: I was soliciting health insurance for Eurydice, courting special education services, trying to negotiate future daycare. Eurydice's father had not acknowledged her as his child and had no plan to provide assistance in the future. The only chance I had of providing for Eurydice while tending to her solo was with a little daycare and health coverage. My neighbor, a doe-eyed French Algerian man, with more jobs on his resume than his thirty-four years, was teaching me how to navigate French bureaucracy.

But more than anyone, it was Eurydice herself—my alarm clock and my accomplice—who was doing the teaching. Her cries unstuck me from my desk chair and unleashed my housebroken thoughts. They also kept depression at arms' length: "Black care rarely sits behind a rider whose pace is fast enough," thought Theodore Roosevelt as he rode his horse into the Badlands after the death of his wife and, the same day, of his mother. My fevered brain teemed with questions, but one thing I knew for sure: When in doubt, keep moving.

Chapter 2

Stress Is The Foundation Of Youth

Eurydice with me on a travel assignment on the Irish island of Inishmore

In the first several months of Eurydice's existence I took her on numerous travel missions—not so much because I wanted to but because travel writing was the only kind of writing I could do with a screaming infant and no daycare. Library research was out of the question. Anything that involved extended amounts of time sitting quietly was out of the question. Sure, travel writing took moments of skimming history tracts and stringing adjectives together elegantly, but there was more motion than meditation required. And meditation was a virtual impossibility with a colicky infant. So the leaps and bounds I could not take philosophically I took physically. I had beloved editors at *Condé Nast Traveler* where I'd spent years writing sporadically, and when I told them I needed to get out of the house while Dice had no help, they were sympathetic. In short succession, they sent us to the haunting Irish island of Inishmore, where Eurydice distinguished herself by curling up to sleep in a drafty hotel drawer every night, the stark East German island of Hiddensee, where she discovered the displeasures of post-communist nudism, and the smoldering Italian volcano island of Stromboli where the black sand set off her pallor like porcelain. I wrapped these trips up as an essay on "Moody Islands" and called it a day.

It was as the ferry was backing away from Stromboli though, that I had an epiphany. I did not want to go home. In many ways, I had no home. I wanted to keep wandering and while I'd made it to a sun-kissed Mediterranean country on company tab, I wanted to at least stay for a while. So I rifled through my travel-diaper-laptop-formula bag, fished out my *Eyewitness Travel* guide to Italy and began flipping hungrily through its pages. I didn't have much money of my own so I needed to stay relatively local. I also needed to reschedule my plane ticket, ideally to travel out of the same town I'd flown into, Naples. And then I saw it: Ischia, a neighbor of Capri. While Capri was trendy and full of millionaires in yachts and overpriced chain shops, Ischia seemed like a gem. A place of healing baths, imposing rocky scenery, turquoise waters and inexpensive lodging. In minutes I was on the phone with *Air Italia* canceling our return flight.

"Okay!" I sighed to Eurydice. "Now we have no plane and nowhere to be! We've got to make ourselves a foothold on an island called Ischia." I would make inquiries when we got to the port in Naples. Surely there would be some possibility of getting there today: the Italians are a sea-faring people, and Ischia is right en route to Capri.

And indeed when we arrived at our port in Naples we spotted a ship with four big illuminated numbers mounted above its deck: 24 00. It was headed for Ischia at midnight. We had only a few hours to entertain ourselves in Naples and no place to call our own, so I placed three-month-old Dice on the port's ancient marble floor, changed out one of her diapers for another, tossed the old one in the public trash bin, and headed toward a simple seafront taverna with menu items like Mozzarella. Period. Melon. Period. Ham. Period. Tomatoes. Period. So we got mozzarella, melon, ham and tomatoes and devoured them with gusto. Alright, Dice ignored the fruit and vegetable group but fared that much better with the mozzarella and meat. When the ship horn began to wail we knew it was time to head off on our 24 o'clock date.

We were no sooner on the top deck of our bobbing vessel than cars began to drive into the bottom and their drivers emerged upstairs looking refreshed. A boat helm beats a windshield any day. Next to us appeared an Italian man with a cage. On further inspection the cage had a cat in it, a big, white, longhaired cat. Eurydice was in the throes of bliss. She had never met an animal she hadn't liked so far and this one was straight out of a fairytale. The stocky, dark-haired owner delighted in Eurydice's attention, and we began to chat.

Where were we going? I didn't know. How were we getting there? I didn't know. Or rather, I did know that I wanted to go to a scenic village called Sant'Angelo and that I hoped to find a bus or cab in that direction and a flea-bag hotel for our first night.

So the predictable happened and the Cat Man persuaded us to ride with him to Sant'Angelo, assuring us that taxis were impossible to find at this hour and buses had stopped. He knew because he lived there. How bad could a man with a furry white cat be? Not bad, I surmised: he seemed a perfect gentleman and a protector of fragile grace. We might place ourselves under his protection with impunity, I concluded as the cat purred. So when the boat creaked to a halt in front of a darkened mound in the sea called Ischia, I descended with Dice, and we piled into Matteo's tiny car. It was 2 am.

His house was on the way to Sant'Angelo, he told us. We would be passing it on our right. He stopped on a pitch-black street. Would we come in for a moment and toast our arrival? I didn't think so, I said; another day. My baby needs to sleep. She can sleep in his house: it has many rooms, said the stranger, and, in any case, we'll talk for only five minutes.

Under the circumstances—no light in sight, empty country road—I could not identify many options but to rely on the good faith of our feline-fond host, so I said yes. Okay. Five minutes: We're tired.

Soon we found ourselves behind a high mossy wall in a sprawling bungalow with nothing but a blaring blue television set for light. Our host mixed drinks in the dark and commented fluently on the reports coming in. Something about the Vatican. He believed in the Vatican. All religions were bad but Catholicism was the least bad. Was I Catholic? No, I said. Why not? he asked suspiciously. I was brought up Protestant and wasn't so clear about religion in general. Wrong thing to say. I think it made me fair game for the Cat Man's darker impulses.

"Where is your child's father?" he asked. "He left," I said. "Was he Asian?" he asked suddenly, leeringly, as though to be Asian was a lascivious, outré thing to be. "No," I said, "he was Greek." "Then why does she have eyes like that?" He looked censoriously at Eurydice's slightly slanted, cat-like eyes. "She has Down syndrome," I said: "She was born with a little disability and kids with that disability all have a bit slanted eyes."

Now my host was looking at me as though I was a truly fallen woman. "So you are not Catholic and you have a baby with Down syndrome," he said as though announcing a death sentence: "Stay here tonight."

"That's very nice of you but we really need to go to Sant'Angelo. Please take us."

"Look at the house; there are many rooms," he said, flinging open doors left and right. "All the hotels in Sant'Angelo are closed now."

"That's okay. We'll walk until we find one—or else we'll just walk," I said a little idiotically.

"I insist you stay here. It is Neapolitan hospitality. Here is your room, all yours." He gestured me into a bedroom.

"I need to go change Eurydice," I said, escaping with my baby to an adjacent bathroom and closing the door.

"May I watch?" he asked eerily, and reopened the door.

"I'd rather you didn't," I said.

"You're not Catholic," he said as though this was relevant.

"Listen, I'm not Catholic but I'm very shy and don't spend nights in the houses of men I've only just met," I said, trying not to offend.

"I'm shy too," he said.

I stood up with the changed Eurydice and tried to

walk past him. He pushed me against the bathroom wall and started to move his pelvis against me.

"No!" I said shoving past him violently and escaping into the small room he had designated to me and locking the door behind me.

"What's wrong with me? Why don't you like me?" he snarled.

"It's me, not you! I do not kiss men I haven't known for long. I am extremely shy," I said like a metronome.

I started to barricade the door with what furniture I could move in the room—two armchairs, a bedside table. My own suitcase. The baby carriage. Is it possible we could make it through a night here? Would he let us out the next morning? Eurydice was strangely mute. All day and night she had colic and now, just as I could perhaps use her crying for help, she was silent as a stone. But then again, I had seen no other residence around; it felt like Matteo's house was on a large property bordered by other large properties with no one close enough to hear a scream.

And then I heard it. A key turning in a lock to an outside door and then being removed. He was locking us in. This was no guileless boor. He was a scheming criminal. It was time to strike before it was too late. Why ever did I have so much stuff? I scanned my suitcase and baby carriage; I would have to abandon them. So with nothing but Eurydice in my arms, my computer bag across my chest and bare feet, I turned the bedroom key in the bedroom door and slipped into the darkened house. Was there an outside lock that he had not gotten to yet? There were a number of plate glass sliding doors—there! There was one that still had a key sticking inside. Swiftly I seized and turned it, and Eurydice and I emerged into the cold night air. Soundlessly, like partners in crime, we tiptoed over paving stones, trying to avoid the rustling leaves on the ground. Soon we were at the iron gate. Easily two meters high, it had spikes. The wall alongside had no footholds—and strategically placed glass shards along the top.

How did I end up in this scrape? It was the scrape a sixteen-year-old might get into. Not that a sixteen-year-old should. But still less a thirty-something year-old mother of a special needs child with the special needs child in tow. When I was sixteen I might have been able to scale the cast iron fence in my skinny jeans and sneakers, to leap to the ground carefully from around the spikes. But now? Barefoot and (still recently) pregnant, with a flowing skirt and a fragile 18 pound bundle of flesh and love on my hip, the idea was absurd. What ironical God had set us up for this? (Not the Catholic one, I gathered.)

I hoisted Eurydice up a few inches on my waist. I reached out for an iron pole, pulled, and—crack!—a twig broke noisily under my foot. "*Eh, bella, che cosa fai?*" came the inevitable voice from the house. *What are you doing, beautiful?* Steps behind me and then … Matteo. *Don't blame him* I warned myself; don't tell him he's a rapist; tell him you're a coward. Assume the blame yourself.

"I'm so sorry," I said disconsolately. "I have never spent the night in the house of a man I've only just met. I'm frightened. Forgive me. It's not *you*. It's *me*."

"What is wrong with me?" he barked.

"Nothing is wrong with you. You're great. I'm just OVER-Catholic. I need to spend the night alone. We can meet another time! But not now, not at night!"

Anything to get out of this place. And anything to make this man not angry at me and Dice now that our lives were in his hands.

"You promise you will see me tomorrow if I let you leave tonight?" he said to my surprise. "I'll find you."

"I promise," I said.

I went to retrieve the suitcase I had thought to abandon and the baby carriage. Matteo opened the door and I walked out. Incredulously. The daylight had arrived by the time we made it to an out-of-the-way *pensione* in Sant'Angelo and pleaded for a room for my daughter and me. The personnel did not have room in the main inn. But they walked us to an empty adjunct building a block and a half away and gave me the keys to a room. It was 6 am. I hoped that it would be the last I saw of Matteo.

The next day was sunny somnolence. I wheeled Eurydice up and down the steep walkways of tiny Sant'Angelo and we got a pass to go to the baths for which the town was renowned. I'd take Dice into the water, float about with her until she squealed with delight, then I'd wrap her in a huge white towel like a mummy and ask the surprisingly willing Italian sunbathers to watch her as I swam. By evening we had a group of friends. Unfortunately I did not yet have their phone numbers.

For by nightfall I would need them. Back in our adjunct hotel after dinner, we heard one, two, three taps on the sliding glass doors to our patio. It was nearly 1 am and it was him. He had climbed over the wall of the building in which Eurydice and I were living alone and he was looking for company. Our quarters were the size of a dressing room—there was nowhere I could escape his eyes. I hurled the curtains shut, sure that he nevertheless had angles on me, and called reception. But reception was closed. There was no phone book and I had no idea how to call the police in Italy—or even the operator. I called random numbers, hoping at least to get another room, a local bar, anything. Nothing. Finally I tried long distance. I tapped two zeroes and a one and called my closest friend, thousands of miles away in California.

"Russell?" I said. "This is going to sound unlikely but I need you to call emergency in Italy. There's a crazy man at my window and I'm alone in this room with no phone book or internet. "

A sharp tug at the glass door and a loud rap. "I only want to talk!" said Matteo. "Let me in! I love you!"

"Then please go away and we'll talk in the daytime," I said to Matteo. Then back to Russell. "I'm in Sant'Angelo on the island of Ischia at the Hotel Verde—or rather at the *adjunct* building of the Hotel Verde."

"I don't know if I'm going to be able to do this," said Russell. "I don't speak any Italian."

"Please!" I begged. "Try. Or at least get me the number for the police in Ischia. It's near Naples."

"I'll try," said Russell as the pleading of my gentleman caller got louder.

Ten minutes later: a miracle. On the front door of my room: a knock. The Ischia police had found me. "The station got a call from America…."

Matteo was gone. The police's lights flooded the neighborhood in vain. I described my assailant.

"He's a Mafioso," they said. "We know who he is. Do not even speak to him; when a woman speaks to him he believes she is his. A lot of Mafiosos are like that."

The patrol men spent the night stationed around our isolated building. The next morning I moved into the main hotel and made friends with a big-hearted foursome of travelers from Naples who warned me about the Mafia in the area and took me under their collective wing. For the next few days I did everything with them; swim, dine, drink, talk, hike, and play with Eurydice, who finally lost her ghostly pallor and looked every moment more like a golden local. When Matteo's head bobbed up in a crowd—as it continued to do at least once a day for the week I remained—my Italian protectors gathered more tightly around me until he disappeared again. I felt safe.

But by the time I returned to Paris I also felt privileged —not merely for the fine weather and fellowship, the sun and security but for the storm and stress. I had been all but certain that motherhood—indeed middle age—would represent the end of adventure, the end of raised heart rates and improbable predicaments. I imagined the life of a parent of a special child to be full only of soporific nursery rhyme refrains and suburban dullness. I was shocked to find that it still contained risk and reality, the necessity of flexibility and the dream of novelty.

The wisdom of our time tells us that stress ages us, but in many ways it's also what keeps us young, on our toes, bendy in body and mind, uncomplacent. Who feels and looks younger: the man in the rocking chair or the man on the swinging rope, the woman in a student room or the woman in an airy mansion? Stress and hardship are as much our friends as they are our opponents; they smooth more lines than they carve. It's the idle aristocrat on the sun-bed who wrinkles the most rapidly, not the resourceful nocturnal hitchhiker—with or without the baby.

I would wager that if one could package it, stress might be among the most successful youth treatments on the market. Its reputation in a good part of occidental society is undeserved. More Western people become fat and stodgy from a settled life than from an unsettled one. "Men wish to be settled," says Ralph Waldo Emerson, "and only so far as they are unsettled is there any hope for them."

Chapter 3
Celebrate Partial Victories

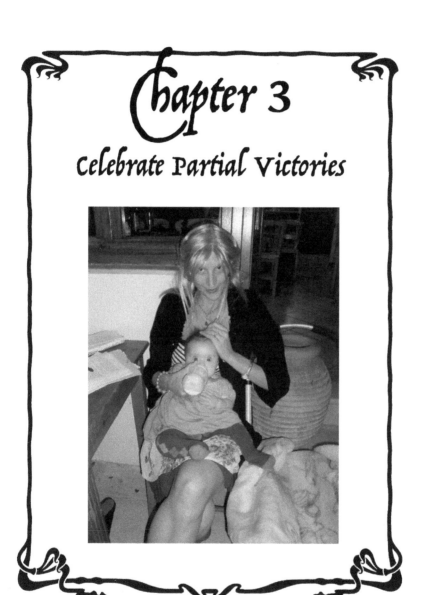

*Eurydice in Chania, Crete where we failed to persuade her
father to provide child support—or any support at all*

My complicity with Eurydice was growing every day. In the evening I talked to her between lullabies and spread out my life dilemmas before her as to a best girlfriend. She stared up at me with her large, dark, long-lashed eyes—she was growing ever more beautiful—and stroked my big hand with her little hand. At night I never ceased to be amazed that she felt secure enough to sleep. I was just an unruly kid at heart, how was it that I could provide an infant with sufficient safety and comfort to make her sleep? I marveled. I celebrated. I watched this still foreign, already deeply loved babe slumber in the crib I'd assembled for her and painted red and pink, and I was charmed. My puerile crafts project, sufficient for the adult task of putting a small human creature to sleep! I felt honored by every even breath Eurydice took, by every stuffed animal she pulled to her cheek, by every sweet smile she directed at me with a yawn in tow.

I could take care of someone! I who had always had

trouble taking care of myself could take care of the most vulnerable of beings, a baby with a serious medical condition—a babe that could not yet talk or crawl but who could smile from ear to ear and scatter light around her as though it was confetti. I was proud. I felt endlessly tender. I knew that whatever happened I would be at this little girl's side.

One day when she was a few months old I resolved to take her to Crete. I wanted to see if there was any chance of her reacquiring the support of her large Greek family. I was proud of her Greek heritage if not of her Greek father, and wanted to give them a chance, Eurydice a chance, to become close. I knew the only way to do this was in person, so I booked a plane ticket and landed in Chania.

Vasilis was where he always was—at his restaurant, *Tamam*. When I arrived he did something extraordinary: he rented an apartment for Eurydice and me in the Old Harbor. It was where I had always wanted to stay, and where he had always forbidden me to seek housing because he preferred the wide, dusty asphalt streets, bigger washing machines, central heating systems and garages of the New Town (never mind that we had no car, that heating was usually redundant in Chania, and small washing machines work as well as large ones for the couple we were). It had been one of our many small conflicts. I felt that if I moved to his town, island and country, he could make the leap to live in a part of that town, island and country that I found appealing. But this was not in Vasili's proud genes. Not until now.

It was with delight that I mounted the spiral wood steps and made my way to the balcony next to the little bedroom above. A Romeo and Juliet balcony—tiny and hovering over the tangled alleys and moonlit cobblestones. I was bewitched. And even as it became apparent that Vasili had no intention of integrating his daughter with his present life—that indeed he had a new girlfriend and vacillated between staying at her house and at his mother's—I remained bewitched. It was my dream come true to live among these ancient yellow walls, among the glow-worm orange lanterns, the hand-painted wooden signs, the bobbing fishing boats, to have this warm stone beneath my bare feet. So what that the context was imperfect? In the past I had had love and no old town. Now I had the old town and no love, boyfriend, or father for my child.

If you wait until you have all the chips together, you will do exactly that: wait. You will wait forever and never rejoice at anything. So I resolved—even as Vasili told me about the sex he had with his girlfriend which prevented him from coming to see his daughter—to be happy, to relish these stolen moments in the heart of Greece's most beautiful old city. I performed the task that Vasili asked me to—he desperately wanted a DNA test since he never trusted that I could be more faithful than he; he was always jealous and every Californian smile I imparted to locals he took as a sign of infidelity—so I did one in a lab nearby, though it hurt me to open Dice's little veins for such a frivolous cause. But Dice seemed okay with everything, happy to be alive, happy to be with me, happy to smile at her father, even while he frowned, happy to head to the beaches with me and lie on the red rocks as we waited for Vasili to join us. The DNA tests came out as everyone knew they would—Vasili was Dice's father—but it made no difference. He did not turn up on the beaches where we arranged to meet. "Where were you?" I would ask, "we waited on Akrotiri beach for hours yesterday."

"Oh well," he would say, "I went to Stavros beach. I walked my dog at Stavros. The dog prefers Stavros." He was punishing me for being right, punishing me for no longer being in love with him, punishing me for presenting him with an imperfect daughter. But I was unpunishable—as we all are when we refuse to participate in the moral oppression of an angry opponent. I pushed Eurydice's soft feet into the soft sand and tried to get her to walk. I sang songs to her over our moonlit balcony, I tried to coax her to say "Good night, sweet Chania! I love you!" and wave her little hand into the dark. *Goodnight Chania, goodnight moon, goodnight night.*

It was a beautiful two weeks in Crete, though we saw almost nothing of Eurydice's father or family. His mother and sister were too intimidated by their golden boy to receive his cast-off girlfriend personally and Vasili himself was too busy with his budding new relationship to risk it by conceding any genuine time to us. I did leave with an ATM card that he said he would put some money on occasionally for his child—but he soon stopped. No matter: It was too little to buy diapers for a month. So I put all this out of my mind, breathed the warm, jasmine scented air, felt the ancient stone underfoot, cried to the moon like a wolf, and cuddled my warm, trusting Eurydice in this city that was hers in spite of it all. If she had faith in the future how could I lack it?

The point, in any case, was not the next chapter. The

point was the present chapter. If in the present we can't enjoy partial victories, we will never enjoy any victories at all—because partial victory is the only kind of victory that actually exists. Dice and I were among some of the most beautiful old walls in the world and we had a connection to them. Dice's ancestors came from these walls, this wind, this earth. Who cares that her father was behaving badly. (Even if he had behaved well he could have helped us very little.) All Dice's other Greek ancestors were around us— in the sage, in the rosemary, in the thyme. We were warm, our nostrils full of sweets. Whatever the future reserved, we were happy in the present. As Jonathan Franzen says, "We are always waiting for the real story to begin, but the only real story is that we die."

Chapter 4

You Are What You See, Not Where You Sit

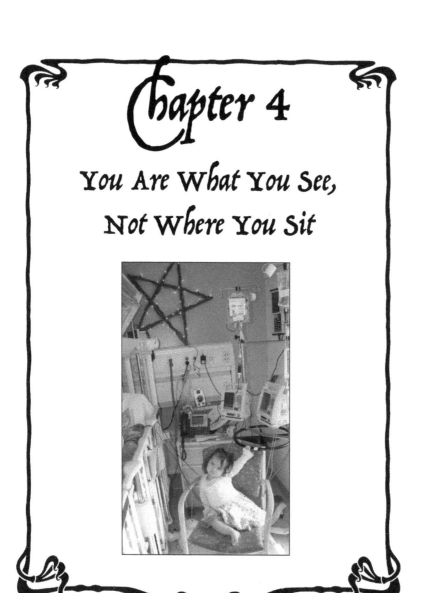

Eurydice, with leukemia, in her "room with a view"
at the UCLA Medical Center

It wasn't long after we returned from Crete and Dice began daycare that she was diagnosed with cancer.

It was supposed to be chickenpox. It was for a chickenpox diagnosis that I went to get blood work done with Eurydice in a lab near her daycare center. A lot of kids had it, and the administrators wanted to know if the little purple dots on Dice's legs and chest were the real thing. They weren't. They were far worse.

The little purple dots that seemed scattered like party glitter over Dice's skin—especially at pressure points like where her carriage straps rubbed against her legs or on her face when her color rose were not pox, but *petechiaie*. The symptoms of bad blood clotting—that is, of low blood platelets. And indeed the numbers spoke for themselves. Kids Eurydice's age are supposed to have between 150 and 450 blood platelets per milliliter, but she had 30.

"We need to repeat the tests," said her doctor, "There must be a mistake; this child does not have leukemia;

I know kids who have, but this is not one of them; she does not fit the profile; she is far too energetic and boisterous. Trust me," she said with the authority of her sixty-something years, "I am an old pediatrician and this child does not have leukemia. We will retake the tests and prove it."

We retook the tests and the Eurydice's platelets were twenty. Then they were ten. Next was a bone marrow test—anesthesia, hammering into Eurydice's back with what looked like mechanic's tools, taking a sample of bone marrow, and analyzing it. But by that time much of me knew it already. It was going to be the worst case scenario. Dice had leukemia. My roly-poly firebrand of a girl had the disease associated with bloodless youths and fainting maidens. It seemed impossible but it was true.

Not entirely true, that is: Eurydice had *developing* leukemia, and it was possible in kids with Down syndrome that developing leukemia could spontaneously regress; after all, the Down syndrome community was known for all kinds of blood anomalies. All we could do is watch and wait. And transfuse. From that day on until the day Eurydice formally entered isolation room chemotherapy several months later, Eurydice had a platelet transfusion a week.

They take a long time, platelet transfusions. Eurydice was attached to a bag that looks like it's full of honeycomb and must wait for four, five hours as this heavy wax-like substance pushes into her veins. This became our Friday routine. And until the following Monday, Dice would have no *petechiaie*. By Thursday she was covered in them. My beautiful girl of the alabaster skin looked like she had been brushed with ashes.

This was a time of frenzied research for me. The moment I found an instant of quiet I would leap online and write leukemia experts on four continents about Eurydice's myelodysplastic syndrome, as her brand of pre-leukemia was called. Some recommended bone marrow transplants, and others recommended chemotherapy, still others experimental protocols. Some—like Eurydice's father, who I managed to reach and ask to check whether his bone marrow was a match for his daughter's—recommended I do nothing. (And *he* did nothing.) This was the last time I talked with him.

The day after Eurydice's first Christmas, she entered the hospital in my parents' town, Los Angeles. My father, a youthful man embarrassed to be a grandparent in the first place and further discombobulated by the circumstances under which he had become one—had stepped up to the plate. He had put Eurydice on his UCLA professor's insurance, consulted, as I did, with UCLA's head of pediatric oncology, and secured Eurydice a financially feasible room at UCLA's children's hospital for the course of an in-house chemotherapy cycle that could take as long as 8 months. So when the bone marrow test Eurydice had when she arrived for her winter break in LA showed 90% leukemia cells—as opposed to the 15% and later 20% the earlier French tests had shown—it was straight down the rabbit hole to Medical Marvel-land.

Instantly, when you get to hospital they try to transform you. Here, put on this faded gown, wear this label around your wrist. Turn yourself into a shapeless mass of patient-hood, shave off your individuality as, in a few weeks, you will your hair. It is easier to treat, easier to lose a person who does not *look* like a person but like an ambulant pin cushion.

I deliberately kept Eurydice's color-saturated clothes on, even when I had to cut pieces from them to make way for different chest catheters into which the chemicals were poured. They could catheterize but they could not color-free her. They could not stamp out her natural flamboyance.

The treatment was punishing, the environment claustrophobic, and the results uncertain. I slept with Dice at night and labored to entertain her in the day. Attached as she constantly was to an IV pole she could not move around her room even in the only form of locomotion she had mastered—the high-speed headlong butt scoot. Never a crawler, Eurydice always looked out and ahead of her as she moved; she never examined the ground, even when it was about to be pulled out from under her. In fact, I think that over the endless months Eurydice and I spent in our hospital isolation room, that was our advantage: Surrounded as we were by IV poles, Kool-aid colored chemo solutions, Hepa-filter air cleaning systems and beeping digital screens, we sat, most often, on an armchair looking out the window. There, in the distance, were trees, birds, blossoms, life. Where around us all was artificial, high-tech, and sterilized, our eyes and souls were outside with unwashed nature, "nature red in tooth and claw" as Tennyson called it. We watched birds fight, fall and sing. Only our buttocks were in custody. Our souls were outside with the squirrels and the trees. You are what you see not where you sit. It is where your eyes are—not your buttocks!—that you really live. A person on a remote island looking at a detergent ad on television is more in the laundry room than in that exotic paradise. The soul is trapped by what it contemplates—and it is also liberated. Dice and I held hands and stared out that isolation room window for all our lives were worth.

Chapter 5

You're No Worse Off After Death Than Before Birth

Eurydice and me in the middle of in-house — and on-horse — chemotherapy

The prognosis was bad. We learned as much on the occasion of Eurydice's one-month bone marrow test. After roughly a month—or cycle—of chemotherapy, the leukemia is supposed to be knocked out. The subsequent five cycles planned were only to make the territory inhospitable for it to come back. Call it the Scorched Earth philosophy of medicine. Except in our case it did not work.

Eurydice took the harrowing marrow test for the fourth time in her little life and we found that the cancer was still there. Diminished, to be sure, by the Shock and Awe campaign that had just been waged on it—a campaign which had nearly killed her—but still there. Since with every cycle of chemotherapy her immune system was destroyed by the chemicals until slowly it reconstructed itself only to be knocked flat again, she was susceptible to every possible infection; a stuffy nose could provoke death. And at the end of the first cycle it almost had. A stuffy nose turned into a high fever which was treated with three kinds of antibiotics, none of which did a thing to improve it, and all of a sudden our room, at 4 am, was full of resident doctors and nurses. They were switching in new IVs and taking blood pressures and Eurydice began to tremble like a leaf. Not tremble, but shake violently as though in the throes of an epileptic seizure. I thought, in all honesty, that it was over. I screamed at the staff for answers.

"It's the amphotericin," said a bulky young doctor I'd never met before on the ward. "It's not for nothing it's nicknamed Ampho-terrible." Amphotericin was a remedy of last resort—a so-called anti-fungal medication that you gave to prevent fatal full body infections or sepses when they were already well under way. One of amphotericin's many possible side effects was seizures. The doctors had not told me what they were giving Eurydice to keep from frightening me. They did not tell me how close they thought she was to the abyss.

As things happened, she skirted it. The fever went down and, after several days, she seemed better. And then we learned the results of the marrow test.

Still cancer.

As unbelievable as everything had been so far since Eurydice's birth, this was more unbelievable than anything. I'm going to be one of those tragic figures, I thought incredulously—a mother whose child died. And then I thought no, no, that is a role I will never play. If Eurydice dies then so do I. I will horde medicines and I will accompany her into death. This child who only a year and a half earlier had seemed a bizarre appendage to my life had since become my lifeblood, my heartthrob, my inseparable accomplice, my heart's darling. There was no way I was allowing her to go somewhere scary without me. I would hold her hand as I was holding it now, look into her eyes, pull her to my bosom and swallow the pills at the same time that she breathed her last few breaths. We would alight in the next world—if there was one—together, hand in hand, as we had confronted so much already. And if there was no other world, we would go into nothingness together. But *together*. She would not be afraid to go anywhere I was going with her, and I would not be afraid of a place that my lovely, unlikely, pudgy, small soul mate was brave enough to go. We would be together. The romance I had dreamt of sharing with a man I would share with my child, my precious, delicate, adored child. And it was all going to be okay.

After all, as Seneca said, it is no more tragic to be gone in one decade than it is to not yet be born in another. In the beginning of 2008, Eurydice was not here yet; was it a tragedy that at the beginning of 2010 she would no longer be here? Was it a tragedy that I wouldn't? Wasn't it the same level of tragedy to not be *yet* than not be *anymore*? And yet nobody would think of bursting into tears because, say, Percy Shelley was not yet born in 1791; why then the moaning when people learned he would no longer be alive in 1823? Non-existence is non-existence.

I thought these things but then I went out and wept. My mother and father covered for me at the hospital, and I went out shopping. My face streaked with tears, my vision blurry, I would buy every toy from which I thought Eurydice could derive any pleasure at all. It was not the quantity of life, but the quality that mattered. And I was going to make her quality of life in that hospital room fabulous. It would be all kisses and cuddle toys and fun. My cherub would smile as she never had before. And then we would drift off together. A lifetime insomniac, I had the sleeping pills to kill a horse at home, and I was going to take them and wander with my Eurydice into the Underworld, not to bring her out again but to comfort her within its valleys.

And yet I kept bursting into tears. Nothing was as sewn and shut as I tried to believe. I came back to Eurydice with arms full of plush animals and then fell to crying like the baby she was and I was not. Never had I felt such deep connection: not with any of the men with whom I imagined absolute union. Here we were, Eurydice and me, a perfectly mismatched pair—a gangly blonde intellectual and a chubby, fine dark-haired cheerleader—and we were perfect. Perfectly in love and prepared to go to purgatory or paradise, being or nothingness, together.

For as I wept Eurydice cheer-led. The moment the fever blisters receded from her mouth and her forehead cooled, she laughed. She blew kisses to the nurses. She tickled them under their arms when they came to give her a hug. "I need my Eurydice fix," said Selena, a favorite. Every morning she dropped in religiously to see us. My dying baby was the source of high spirits and high fives in a ward that can grow silent with its solemn charge.

It was hard to believe. And then the tide turned.

Chapter 6

Eschew Competitive Suffering

Eurydice continuing chemotherapy with her mother on location 24/7

Eurydice's cycles started getting less draconian. Normal infections were treated with the normal series of antibiotics, and hope, somehow, was in the air. I wandered into the medical center cafeteria one day while my mother watched Dice in the afternoon and thought to myself how good it was that Ampho-terrible seems to have been struck off Dice's shortlist. At that moment a woman rifled in front of me and hissed, "I have no time to wait in line, I have a 16-year old on IV antibiotics upstairs."

I couldn't suppress a smile.

"There's nothing to laugh about young lady," came the cold retort.

"It's just that I have a one-year-old on three kinds of IV antibiotics—and on chemo too—upstairs. There aren't many of us in the hospital for the coffee." There were some approving harrumphs in the back of the line among the people before whom the lady had cut, but I swiftly wished I'd kept silent. I was playing a puerile game of one-up-man-ship with this woman: My kid is sicker than your kid. My sick kid is younger than your sick kid. In my irked little mind I twittered on: Your kid's sixteen! Does he even still belong in a children's hospital? Mine's *one*. And has *cancer*. Not some lowly throat infection. So stop pulling rank, lady.

It is ironic how our sufferings—instead of sensitizing us to the sufferings of others—can instead make us defensive and territorial. There are few things we protect as vigilantly as our little squares of suffering. Not even our accomplishments we guard as jealously as our injuries. If I am injured, I want the world to know. And if the world is not eager to listen because it is nursing its own wounds, why I'll beat it over the head. I'll cut in line, or stomp, or curse.

We can take a lot of pain as long as it is acknowledged. But when it is downplayed or overlooked, we call to arms. It is heartbreaking that those often least able to provide the empathy we so need are fellow sufferers. It is as though we thought it was a zero sum game—your hurt makes mine appear smaller. The moment has long come to realize that pain—like love—comes in endless shapes and sizes and affects the lot of us democratically. Then perhaps abused children would not so regularly become childbeaters; we would not wish to pull rank with our injuries so much as use them as wedges into the secret experience of our neighbor.

The woman who had cut in line suddenly turned to give me a hug. "I'm sorry," she said, "I wish your daughter the very best." Before I had unwrapped my sack lunch she was back. In her arms she carried a sparkling tinsel teddy bear from the hospital gift shop. People, I thought to myself, have big hearts. They need their wounds honored. But then they delve into those very wounds and emerge with love. I asked the woman's room number and later that day delivered a huge helium Superman to her son.

Chapter 7

Intelligence Is Overrated

Eurydice on a rare excursion to the hospital lobby

Eurydice and I received visits, day by day, from her grandparents and my friends. She shrieked with glee at the arrival of these visitors—so much so that I dreaded their departure would darken her spirits. "Bye bye, Eurydice," they would croon blithely after an hour, and then the two of us would be left alone again in our little cell.

One amazing thing about Eurydice is that she never mourned. She always feted the arrival of our friends, but she never bewailed their departure. Within moments afterward, she was covering me with kisses and pointing excitedly at the VCR on which we had watched *Dirty Dancing* thirty-five times.

I wonder, in some ways, if this has to do with intelligence. We live in a culture that idolizes a narrowly defined intelligence without criticism or qualification. All parents want their children to go to the best universities, the best nursery schools—and it is never questioned whether the intelligence touted there may not be as frivolous, fuzzy, fashion-dependent (not to mention unearned) a quality as beauty.

What is intelligence? Eurydice, in her hospital room, blathers on in her own jargon; she does not repeat a single word though she repeats gestures aplenty.

An admiring nurse commented that she was "so high-functioning"—but truthfully, I don't even know what that means. In many ways, she is low-functioning. Kids with Down syndrome half her age are already speaking. In truth, I've made language acquisition hard for her by catapulting her into my international existence—an existence that accommodates equal parts of English and French, a good deal of German, and some occasional Greek, Italian and Arabic to boot.

Presumably intelligence has something to do with problem solving. But it's hard to review cultural or literary history without seeing that the most intelligent people have often been the worst at solving their own problems—plainly, the most miserable. Yes, Kafka could think his way through castle labyrinths, but could he figure out what to say to the girls he loved? Or to his father? It is routinely the case that our brightest thinkers are our darkest personalities. Their intelligence makes them eternally unsatisfied, nostalgic or cynical: Rather than helping them solve real-life problems it helps them exaggerate them.

Eurydice is the opposite. She does not live in fear of the future or in nostalgia for the past. When her grandmother whom she loves leaves, she shouts goodbye and a moment later has forgotten her presence—until she returns again, at which point Eurydice treats her to an explosion of festivities. "Yeahhhh!" exclaims Eurydice and claps her hands together.

She lives entirely in the here and now and makes the most of it, neither missing nor forgetting anyone when they are absent and celebrating *every*one when they are present. Her psyche serves to procure greater happiness for those around her (who are spared parting tears but lavished in return celebrations) as well as for herself.

It is as though she knew, with Paulo Coelho, that "the people we love are always there; they are in the same train but in a different coach. It is not because you cannot access the coach that their feelings or your feelings will change. Keep enjoying the journey and try to take the best from the people who are sharing it with you."

It may be Eurydice's deficit of conventional, corrosive intelligence and surfeit of emotional, upbeat intelligence that makes her capable of all this.

The saddest people I have known have been intellectuals. The happiest person I have known is Eurydice. Perhaps it is time we stop worshipping SAT scores and we begin understanding the virtues of affection and acceptance; the ability to take life as it comes, a moment at a time, with all the scintillating lights (or restful shadows) that these moments bring.

Conventional intelligence, like conventional beauty, is an outdated phenomenon. Arbitrarily conferred, often actually disadvantageous, it is eclipsed by simple things like good will, the capacity for joy and for empathy

We are often asked with what major historical or literary figure we would most want to spend a day. There are many, for me—Emerson, Nietzsche, Hazlitt, Simone de Beauvoir—but in all candor the one I most want to spend a day with is Dice. Her happy gestures are worth a thousand words.

Chapter 8

The More You Do,
The More You Can Do

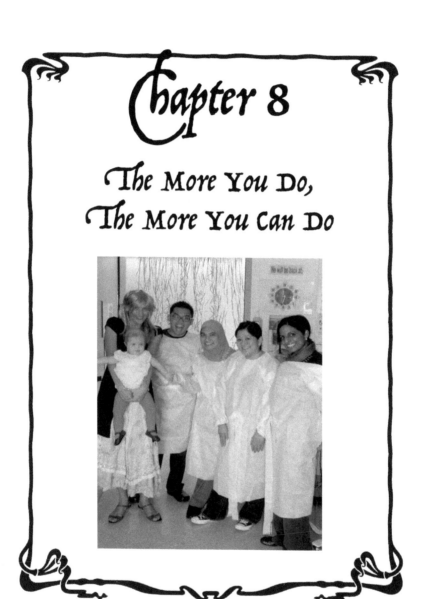

*Dice celebrates her second birthday with the wonderful
nurses on the Pediatric Oncology Ward at UCLA*

If someone had told me less than a couple of years before that I would become mother to a severely handicapped child who would develop leukemia and with whom I would be locked up in an isolation room for seven months non-stop, I think I would honestly have committed suicide. The claustrophobia! The fear! The thanklessness of raising a child who won't be a genius (or even independent)! The prospect would have made me sick to the stomach and ill at heart.

And the reality, I'll admit, was not easy. Things I didn't ordinarily think about drove me crazy. The incessantly bleating machines. The constant huffing and puffing of the Hepa-filter, designed to keep the air clean. The constant need to entertain my baby. It is not as though I could hand Eurydice a book to read or blocks to play with on the floor. She wasn't even allowed on the floor. Germs were the name of the game and she had to play hide and seek with them all the time. So here she was, sitting in a hospital cot barely bigger than she was, unable to sleep, and bored to tears. So I had to dance and prance and make funny faces and read *Dr. Seuss* and point out pigeons outside her window and tickle her. Not even mealtimes provided structure to our day as Eurydice could not eat because of the fever blisters in her mouth and esophagus. It was pure claustrophobia punctuated by fear. And yet I tried to be all smiles so that Dice would keep her spirits up too.

And she did. Exhausting as it was to entertain her, it worked. The child was always in good spirits—so much so that medical staff came by for breaks in their otherwise often relentless rounds of misery.

I still don't know how Dice and I did it—and I would not want to do it again, ever—but what I did realize is that, as William Hazlitt said, "The more you do, the more you can do—

Our capacity is invigorated as it is called out by necessity. By lying idle, as by standing still, we are confined by the same narrow round of topics: by continuing our efforts as by moving forwards in the road, we extend our views and discover continually new tracts of country.

New tracts of country is right: Dice and I figured out how to obtain a floor mat on which she could conduct her trademark butt scoot; we found resources in ourselves we did not know existed. I, who during my university days, had been unable to sit still for a boring lecture, found I had enormous reserves of patience. Dice, who even then was used to changing scenery and abundant travel, found she had great stocks of creativity and could amuse herself endlessly with a piece of yarn. Because of Dice's unique antibiotic immunities, she was never let out from her room. So the two of us sat at the window and gazed longingly at the flowerbeds outside, at the trees and at the cars and the asphalt, the grit and the grime. Anything besides the antiseptic white linoleum prison to which we were consigned.

And then one day was the last. Then one day, we got out.

Chapter 9

Play Wounded

Eurydice, post-leukemia

The day we got out of isolation room chemotherapy, Eurydice and I headed straight for an empty, overgrown lot near the hospital. We straddled the broken down barbed wire fence. And starved as we were for dirt, we dug our fingers deep into the ground, brushed our cheeks against the long, grown weeds and all but gobbled up the dandelions. "Yummmm," said Eurydice, chewing on a stem. It was *so good* to be out of our plastic prison, we would have eaten the earth if we could have. Mud! Insects! Scented stalks of grass! It was paradise. I don't think anyone can imagine how delightful nature is to those deprived of it for many months. I would have stuffed bugs into my bra I was so happy to see them. Creepy, crawly, natural things after all that aseptic smoothness.

Of course, we weren't really supposed to be digging holes in the earth and waking up ringworms. We were supposed to be keeping Eurydice very sheltered in spite of the fact that the post-chemo blood counts were encouraging—meaning that her immune system was slowly beginning to normalize. But it simply felt like such a party, being able to reunite with the elements: I felt like quoting Whitman at full volume: "Loafe with me in the grass, loose the stop of your throat/Limitless are leaves stiff or drooping in the fields/And brown ants in the little wells beneath them!"

Eurydice forced her little knuckles into the ground. Digging among the grass and the ants was heaven.

But of course we returned to hospital for a post-chemo bone marrow test and it was—once again—ambiguous. There were a number of young immature cells—which could be leukemic cells. After weeks of study, the specialists came down on the side of victory; the young cells were an anomaly, not a sign of recurring cancer. But never again will I take Eurydice's health for granted. Always, every day, I give thanks for it. Like all of our lives, hers is fragile. Like all of us, she plays wounded.

The important thing is that she plays—to the hilt— day after day.

Chapter 10

Ignore Well-Meaning Idiots

*Eurydice back at home in our tiny Paris flat,
donning my underwear as a scarf*

W e had just gotten off our transatlantic flight from Los Angeles and arrived in the courtyard of the little Paris apartment building we called home. I was maneuvering Dice's baby carriage across the cobblestones with one hand and dragging our immense orange suitcase behind us with the other. And I met the concierge. A tiny, efficient Portuguese woman, she immediately welcomed me back— and asked if two-and-a-half-year-old Dice could walk.

"No," I said, truthfully, "but she's just come out of seven months of chemo and she's beat childhood cancer."

"Oh," said the concierge, unimpressed. "You know there are homes for children like her."

"This is her home," I said tilting my head toward our apartment.

"I mean homes where she will be taken off your hands," said the concierge. "Where you can finally get your life back."

I dropped my suitcase and bent down over Eurydice's

baby carriage to kiss her hair. "This is the only life I want," I said.

The concierge looked at me ironically and told me she could give me some addresses.

"147 Rue du Temple is our address," I said. "Thank you so much though."

Shaken, I locked Eurydice's baby carriage onto the stairwell railing, extracted her from her seat and began to carry her up the weather-beaten stairs.

It was a grim welcome after a grim sojourn. Dice had fought for and won her life but apparently not her place in French society. And this in spite of the fact that it was plain to all with eyes to see how loved she was. Not that my love was her redemption; she was her own redemption.

As I bid goodbye to the concierge, Eurydice high-fived her and called "bye byyyye" in her bright voice.

It took me days to get over this reception.

But Dice wasn't bothered in the least. She saw the woman's good intentions and proved indifferent to their content. Not for the first time, I saw how very, very much I had to learn from my little daughter.

Chapter 11

Trust Strangers

Eurydice and me in a Paris park celebrating
after the reacquisition of our handicapped papers

The fluorescent white light flashed over small Eurydice's face.

"Beautiful," I said, and caught the picture as it wafted into the Photomaton's delivery slot. I pulled back the brown curtain separating us from the commuters pounding past in the Republique metro station.

"We're done, Dice. You're a star."

The ID photo was the last item we needed to complete a "Handicapped Package" I had been laboring to assemble ever since Eurydice and I had returned to Paris after her cancer treatment in Los Angeles.

It had taken weeks to gather the diagnoses, birth certificates, charts, passports, proofs of paternal abandonment and assessments for this file. French bureaucracy is opaque to all but French bureaucrats. And even they only stare through the glass darkly.

In any case, I "had it all" now—if that's how you can describe having an over-stuffed envelope proving your child has only 10% of her marbles in the eyes of the state. The French government considers Eurydice "90% handicapped."

Still perched on the Photomaton's swivel stool and now spinning and squealing at top volume, Dice seemed nothing at all like a tenth of a child. She seemed more like ten children. I had to quiet her down. It was time for her baby bottle which I'd crammed into my backpack alongside my laptop whose keyboard was sticky with milk. But the backpack was flung behind the swivel chair. To retrieve it, I had to retrieve Dice first.

"Come on, sweet," I said heaving her up and out of the booth and maneuvering her gingerly into the carriage which I'd parked just adjacent and which I had dragged down two flights of stairs.

"Coo-coo!" Dice was gesticulating at someone who was gesticulating back at her. Grateful for the child-friendliness of my adopted country people, I looked where she was facing.

At a turnstile just behind me, three young men were waving antically and calling "Bonjour, Petite." I smiled at them, released the stroller brake and pushed Dice back over the threshold of the photo booth so I could reach back in for the backpack.

The backpack was not there. My breath quickened. It must be on my back already. No. I tapped my clavicles; my shoulders were bare. Behind me? Had I, in fact, retrieved it before retrieving Eurydice? Had the men seen something? They were still cooing at her. Actually, no, only one of them was still cooing. The other two had slipped on past the photo booth and were in fact sprinting toward a subway crossing in the distance, toward another part of Paris. "Hey! Stop!" I shouted.

I'd heard people holler "Stop, Thief!" in Paris before— and it had always struck me as both extraordinarily admirable and altogether out of my temperamental range. I shot a pleading look toward the final remaining of the three "bonjour"-sayers—"Did you see someone take my backpack?" I stammered.

Suddenly, he seemed to speak no French. "Hm?" he shrugged at me blankly, and turned to jump over the turnstile behind him.

What could I do? Unwieldy with an oversize baby carriage and a now crying child, could I start a high-speed chase? I took a lame couple of gallops after the two men I now realized had snatched my backpack out of the photo booth while the third continued to distract me. But it was no use. I floundered instead to an information desk and saw a look of profound fatigue descend on the attendant's face as I began to describe what happened.

"I need to get help," I said. "I have a sick baby. And no house key to get her home. No phone, no money, no ID."

"Your husband will let you in, won't he?" murmured the attendant and turned back to a customer who was requesting a subway map.

"I have no husband!"

I heard myself sounding hysterical. "Not even my neighbors are home this month." It was August: Paris's usual population was out of town on vacation.

And then it came over me, wave after sickening wave: "My book manuscript was in that pack too," I started to sputter. "On my computer. I'm a writer, and my next book was in that pack," I explained nonsensically. Commuters stopped and stared at a grown woman carrying on about a book.

"But look, it's my baby who needs help right away," I resumed. "She's disabled. She just got out of chemo. I only took her here because we needed an ID photo...." My voice trailed off.

That ID photo now lay forlornly in the lower basket of the baby carriage.

It was the only thing we had left in the country.

We spent that night in the police station of the Third arrondissement, a characterless modern block dwarfed by a black brick furnace at its side called *Le Depot*, known for the quick and impersonal sex you could have there.

Service in the police station was no more personal, but certainly less quick than at *Le Depot*. As Eurydice wailed, the glazed-eyed officer took drags of a cigarette, snuffed it out, lit a second, asked me to repeat the information I'd provided, lit a third, crossed out what he'd written, lit a fourth, crunched the entire scribbled document into a ball, seized a new piece of paper, started over, lit a fifth cigarette.

"Don't be so exercised," he told me. "This happens every day, all day."

It was midnight before a woman officer gave me 60 centimes to buy milk from the station's vending machine with which I quenched Eurydice's parched tongue. She was not yet able to drink from a carton, and there was no baby bottle to be had at that hour.

It was 1 in the morning by the time I started searching for people I knew in the phone directory at the dispatcher's desk and leaving apologetic little messages on their phones. Just as I turned helplessly to the locksmith section, I saw an apparition: a dashing, dark-haired gentleman standing in the door of the police station. It was a neighbor. And he was clutching, a bit awkwardly, a large bottle of infant formula.

"I'm just back from Marrakech," said Daniel. "I heard your telephone message and let myself into your apartment by slipping a foot X-ray into your lock.. Good thing I sprained my ankle last year. I'll show you how you do it." He motioned toward the door, "Let's get out of this dump."

"Did you actually walk past *Le Depot* with that?" I asked as Eurydice lit up and lunged for her foamy bottle. At that hour and place, my spry gay neighbor was more likely to be taken for a fetishist than a family man bringing supper to a child.

"Mixed it too. And *tasted* it." Daniel's eyes glinted. "It's not one of those drinks I know by heart yet."

I flung myself into my neighbor's thin arms and pressed back tears. Why had he not just pretended to still be in Morocco? It could have been so much less trouble for him.

...

The next month was dedicated, hour by painstaking hour, to the reestablishment of Eurydice's and my official existence in the world. Both our American and European passports had been stolen: As luck would have it, I had taken all four to the xerox shop to make copies for the disability application before I headed to the metro for photos. So off we lumbered to embassy after embassy after embassy. We stood in lines for minors, lines for adults, got frisked, solicited forms, filled them out, brought them back, re-ordered credit cards, exchanged door locks, requested new keys made, repurchased a laptop computer with an American keyboard (wait-time three weeks), grieved silently for my lost manuscript, and belatedly—with Daniel's technical assistance—set up external hard drives to safeguard future writings.

But this only got us back to zero. When almost everything else was said and done—or at least underway—I turned to the most thankless task of all: the reassembling of the baroquely complicated disability file that had been the cause of this entire catastrophe. Eurydice's continued life-saving health coverage depended on the acceptance of this file. Her daycare possibilities depended on it too—as would, soon, any kindergarten that provided the necessary assistance. If you're handicapped in Paris, you can't do much for long without handicapped papers.

So I began again to make little piles on my desk of required documents. After several weeks of this, I was heading out the door to mail another request for a new application form, when I noticed an envelope in my letter box. Tearing it open absently as I continued up the street, I scanned its opening:

"Congratulations. Your handicapped application materials have been received and are soon to be validated! Missing from your application packet are the following materials only: (See below.)"

Down the page a bit, a box was checked: "Your child's ID picture."

Just one item. Everything else had been received.

I stopped in the middle of the cross-walk, pedestrians shuffling by and into me. I stared at the letter in my hands. I read it again. Was it possible?

Was it possible that the thieves—one or all of the thieves—had found the almost completed dossier; read it; felt bad for Eurydice and me; bought stamps out of their own pockets, stuck them onto the 1-kilo packet; and then sent it on its way to the Handicapped Office of Paris?

There seemed no other way to account for the receipt of my stolen application.

And all of a sudden, everything that had happened before this felt tiny. The theft. The loss of my ID, computer, keys, phone. I had just received in their stead one of the most heartening insights about human nature I could possibly have been offered: that it is good.

Even its worst representatives are good. Hardened hit men. Subway robbers who steal from disabled babies. To be sure, they steal—and run—and lie—and cheat – and hurt—and injure—to survive. And sometimes just because the temptation is stronger than they are. But at bottom even *these* individuals, these outcasts of society, these persons who at least partially know they are at least partially bad, they are open to influence, to empathy, to responsibility and kindness. They do good where it is invisible. They do good where no one rewards them. They do good for no other reason than to put more goodness into the world.

It was at that moment that I decided very firmly to reject the easy cynicism of the Paris street.

I would see the remorseful thief in the menacing

gangs that paced through the metro. I'd try to address the would-be hero inside the hooded delinquent, the one who cared if he dared, who wants to do the right thing even when circumstances, habit, and despair often make him do the wrong one.

We don't live in a big, cruel city any more that we live in an isle of inviolate saints. We live, in fact, in a city full of Secret Love, a world shot through with the secret desire to aid, cheer, and bail out our broken neighbors.

"There is so much more good will in the world than is generally believed," said Ralph Waldo Emerson in the 19th century. "How many times in our daily lives do we fail to express the admiration we feel for another from fear of appearing awkward, self-serving, perverted or even dangerous?"

How many of our more generous impulses go repressed? How many of our kinder sides go veiled and invisible? How often do we hide our bleeding hearts and thrust our hardened poker faces ahead of us into the world?

It is so much easier to lament the badness by which we are also surrounded than to admit and attend to the authentic goodness.

It took Dice and the subway robbers of Republique to help me see that just below the shiny surfaces of our sprawling metropolis is not only rot and darkness but gold.

Chapter 12

Stop Waiting Your Turn

Eurydice and Russell

It was always complicated to have a love relationship with Dice around. Of course, I had my near, dear Russell, but he caused me almost as much pain as joy. He was unstable in every romantic way, even while being extremely stable as a friend. During our over ten year love relationship before Dice's birth, we had not only bought engagement and wedding rings and begun to plan three separate weddings in three countries (Scotland, France and the United States), but he had broken with me repeatedly. He never explained why other than to say he was "anxious" in my company; I was either "too fragile" or "too successful" or, my favorite, we had a "different notion of time and space." Every time, I was on the brink of collapse and every time we came back together again, like magnets. I cannot reasonably account for this except to say that Russell's conversation, love, and literary companionship were pivotal to me. He was the older writer, the idol and mentor I never had. And—as Russell says—I was "the love of his life," though he never knew how to respond to this adequately.

So the time came—and came again—that I realized "I need to get out of this relationship that is tearing me apart." When I was in the cancer ward with Dice, I wryly imagined taking out an ad on a dating site: "Mother of leukemic infant with Down syndrome seeks hospital-adjacent partner." Once I got out of the cancer ward I actually did place an ad: I swallowed my pride and asked for a man to accompany me and my daughter island-hopping across the Adriatic and Mediterranean and Ionian sea—no sex.

No one even remotely enticing responded to my platonic invitation. The line between daring and absurdity is air thin—it all depends on the result—and I came down squarely on the side of absurdity. But I resolved to take Eurydice on my own—and, I daresay, learned to live.

I learned to live by banishing the old comfort blanket we all cuddle more or less continually: the threadbare notion of a better tomorrow, superior circumstances in the future, predictable improvement over time. This does not mean that I ceased to believe in the war on poverty or in scientific advancements. What it meant was simply this: My own little life was not going to get easier anytime soon. Having made it through chemotherapy, Eurydice's lung, kidney, heart and immune system were damaged for good. If she ever got out of diapers (a number of kids with DS don't for over a decade), dementia would soon begin to cast its shadow on the horizon (it can start in the twenties with DS). If she learned to walk I would soon have to worry about "bolting"—running away—a frequent source of disaster for DS kids. If she mastered her first spoken words, her first page of reading would be a thousand times harder. If she was cute as a button now, she might be shapeless and stigmatized as an older person.

The future was not golden, so what I decided was that Dice and I would squeeze the flavor out of every second we had on earth. I threw myself headlong into showing her the world. It did not matter that I had no money; it did not matter I had no ready accomplice. I set out on my own with Dice, who I discovered was the gamest travel companion a girl could have—even if she left trails of broken glass in her wake. She embodies good luck. Because good luck is what you create, I now believe, when you *stop waiting your turn*, when you give up your anesthetizing belief that the best is yet to come.

Even if your child does not happen to have cancer or a genetic disability, I am willing to bet that the best is *not* to come. The best is here, in the palm of your hand. As my favorite thinker of the here and now, Ralph Waldo Emerson, once wrote: "Thou art sick, but shalt not be worse, and the universe that holds you dear shall be the better." Yes, you are handicapped. But tomorrow you won't throw off your chains and crutches, recipient of some biblical miracle, you'll just have more.

So I tried to live in the moment—to embrace my flawed companions, knowing that my companions in the future would be corpses. Thanks to my daughter—with her regular post chemo bouts of pneumonia and constant pedagogic challenges, I ceased to "Just say no"; I said "Yes." Far from postponing projects to the mythic day that "the children will be out of the nest" or the income is there, the time is right, the perfect companion is on call, I'm doing them now. But it has taken the guru in the crib to teach me the lessons of the gurus I once studied in graduate school.

"Perhaps it is too soon," Simone de Beauvoir used to tell me from the pages of her journal, *Force of Circumstance*, "but tomorrow it will be too late." My daughter has taught me to hear these sages; her anomaly has put blood into their words. If we could attend her simple lesson, *Hoc opus, hic labor est ("This is the task, this is the labor")*—and stop bargaining for and hypnotizing and consoling ourselves with the future (that false panacea), we would live lives far richer. We'd rush to the middle of the court, the heat of the battle. We'd eat dessert first—and realize this is neither a recipe for weight gain (you skip the potatoes afterward), nor is it self-indulgent; it's simply clear-eyed living. Our opportunity for joy and achievement is right here.

Dice and I booked a charter flight to Morocco soon after we got out of chemotherapy and landed alongside a magnificent walled town called Essaouira. An airport had only just been built in the region; there were still few visitors. We stayed in a windy room at the top of a Medina and looked out over the seagulls and lived to the rhythm of the calls to prayer five times each day.

We walked along the city seawalls, little Dice and me, and often climbed over them into the tumultuous sea. I would sit Eurydice on the top of the wall, climb over it myself and pick her up from the other side. Then we would dip a foot in the water and most often push off the rocks into the sea, me holding the unfrightened Eurydice as the waves sloshed over us. My girl was fearless and was starting to teach me to be fearless too.

We had a suitor in Essaouira, a handsome long-locked local who kept inviting us to his mother's house. Finally, we went. We bounced across the countryside in the back of an extremely rusty pickup truck to what I can only call a matriarchal farmhouse. There was our friend's mother, his grandmother, his grand-aunt, his sister, all dressed in spectacular gold and lavender, pink and orange and magenta headscarves and jellabas (a Westerner in their company did not seem liberated but intensely conservative and mousey)—and sitting on the carpeted floor prepared to give me mint tea. My fear of being kidnapped immediately dissipated.

We stayed the afternoon, wandering among the goats and the olive trees and helping with the laundry. At the end of the day, Yacine asked me to marry him. I flushed scarlet and assured him we would remain friends but I was not the marrying sort. He took it in stride, drove us to the airport and said we would meet again. We haven't done so yet. But his proposal rekindled my faith in romantic love.

Chapter 13

Don't Take a Straight Line Anywhere

Eurydice overlooking the Sahara

W hether it was because of the caretaker of the apartment or not, Eurydice started not only to walk, within weeks of arriving in France, but to bolt. One day she got up on her two wobbly legs, and from then on she never stopped using them. And she never used them timidly either. There were a few weeks left before she could go to daycare, so I planned a trip with her to Tunisia. Disparaged by many French people as an erstwhile colony and a nation of sand and servile waiters, it intrigued me immensely.

Eurydice and I disembarked in Zarzis, just off the southern island of Djerba, set up a base in an extraordinarily spacious, floral and inexpensive hotel and planned our adventures from there. First of all, we would go to the edge of the Sahara—to a place called Matmata, where *Star Wars* was filmed long ago. Littered with craters and strange pyramid-shaped stone formations, it was as lunar a landscape as I could imagine. We hitchhiked there in the back of a dilapidated pick-up truck, the wind in our hair and the shouts of lanky Tunisian youths in our ears. It was a moment that the American embassy had closed in Tunisia, and Americans were warned away from the country: the terrorist threat level was considered too high.

But Dice and I had inveterate faith in our host country and we also believed—or I believed—that our total trust might ingratiate us to people we met. My instinct proved correct. Our host and hitchhiking companions proved nothing but kind and gracious to us; they left us off where we wanted to be left off, bought us a bottle of water, and were gone.

The tricky part ended up being on site. Dice's new-found hiking skills proved devastating. We could be crossing a crater or a thin ledge, but Eurydice could never walk a straight line. Her curiosity was too much for her. Between points A and B she would manage to hit X, Y, and Z. It was exhausting. But I will also admit: It was exciting. We avoided all the tourist tracks and traps. Between a vista point and a bench we managed to do kilometers of bushwhacking, tree stump perching, well tapping and—yes—roof climbing, We forged our own paths through the wilderness, and they were beautiful. Tiring, indeed, but terrific.

When we hitched back to Zarzis, we were beat. But happy.

For the first time in our lives we were not so much mother and daughter but girlfriends. Unlikely girlfriends exploring improbable sites with unseemly enthusiasm.

Chapter 14

Love Is The Noblest Form Of Weakness

Eurydice on the kitchen counter

It was "a dark and stormy night" in Paris, and Eurydice spoke her first entirely correct English sentence.

Nobody could have claimed the circumstances were propitious. Dice was striking Marilyn Monroe poses on her changing table before bedtime. (Regrettable News Flash: kids with Down syndrome need night changing until hell freezes over.) And she decided to thrust her pudgy little hands straight into the glass-framed painting over her head. Well, the glass cracked and so did the skin on her fingers. Her helicopter mom tried to make light of the situation by lowering the lamps in the bedroom, but when blood started to swell like maroon poppies on Dice's ivory nightdress, I gave up the good fight and heaved my child off her changing table and onto the garishly lit kitchen counter where, Help me Lord, I discovered the Red Sea gushing from two index fingers.

Quickly, I scrambled after the masking tape I'd last used to stop a mouse hole and dug up the makeup swabs last used when I last wore make-up. I wound the two wildly around the bleeding digits: Presto! Dice looked like a puzzled saint risen from the grave and admonishing her faithful with two gleaming white over-sized index fingers. She scrutinized these fingers, holding them up near her eyes. In solidarity, I held up my own two index fingers. Then I started to move them around : "I. Love. You," I signed to the saint on my kitchen counter.

It was then that the miracle occurred. She did it. Dice—who has not breathed a complete sentence in the first six years of her life—raised her bandaged hands, signed and simultaneously pronounced "I. LOVE. YOU." She said it once. She said it twice. Four times. She got the "L." She got the "Y." She laughed out loud. She flung her Lazarus arms around my neck and said it again, this time with no signs.

I don't know if it will happen again tomorrow. Breakthroughs in kids with Down syndrome are not reliably replicable in the short term. But this night, unlike any other nights, Dice did it. She said her first English sentence—and it happened to be "I love you." This was something like when she made her first "speech sound" three years ago and it happened to be a kiss. It's slow, yes. But I'll be damned if it ain't the Sweetest Slow I know.

With "kiss," "I love you," and "NO!" in her working vocabulary, the girl's almost ready for the big screen. Which is what she wants. Give her a microphone and she will climb onto the highest object in any room and sing her heart out. Give me a microphone and I'll duck for cover, stumbling in all likelihood over the electric cord as I go. No matter. There can only be one real star in a family of two and Dice is it.

It frightens me sometimes that I love her so much. Love puts you at maximal risk. It makes you vulnerable; it makes you helpless. Anything that happens to Dice would throw me altogether off course. And so much happens to her—from leukemia to late-night bloodletting. But if I have learned anything at all in the past six years I have learned, with George Eliot, that "To have in general but little feeling is the only security against feeling too much on any particular occasion." Life is a series of trade-offs— and in this one I will go with feeling too much rather than feeling too little.

Not that I have a choice.

Chapter 15

Love Grows By Service

Eurydice just before bolting off into the Parisian wilderness

Who is it we love? Is it the one from whom we take most or the one to whom we give most? In my relationship with Eurydice—as in my relationships to certain lovers—I have gleaned the impression that it is the person to whom you give most to whom—ironically—you owe most.

Salespeople know this, in part. They know that you will treasure a stone more if you have paid thousands for it than if you have paid dozens. Casanovas know this: they know that they appreciate a girl more if they have had to court her for long than if they have won her right away.

Our own service is its own reward. And the fact that I am always lobbying for Eurydice, that I sing her praises and her potential at every school meeting, that I chase her down every street where she begins to bolt, makes me not more fatigued in her company but, overall, more energized.

We only know how much we can do when it is demanded of us that we do it. If someone had told me some years ago that I would have a daughter for whom I would have to lobby every moment at school, who would still need diapers at night after seven, eight years, who would not be able to walk up the street with me without disappearing into every courtyard, mounting every wall, and hiding in every bush, I think I would have expired on the spot.

The devoted mother was not my vision of myself by a long shot. But now I realize that a mother is no different from a lover—the more you are asked to give, the more you realize the worth of what you have.

It's an evening in summer, and Eurydice and I are in a bistro having dinner with several friends. "She never stops moving," says the ten-year-old son of a girlfriend.

"No," I say. "She's always in action. The worst is when she dashes off and you can't find her."

My friends chuckle indulgently. "Ah, the worry we put up with for our children," says one, thinking, no doubt, that I'm a touchingly overprotective mother. When it's time to turn in for the night, we scramble around our seats to retrieve our bags and suddenly Eurydice is gone. Eurydice, who was sitting in the middle of the six of us.

"Eurydice!" I say, knowing that when she escapes she never answers.

"She must be in the bathroom," says my friend's little boy.

"Can you go look?" I said, knowing that I myself was going to where the risk was greatest: outside the restaurant.

I swing open the heavy door and address the people on the terrace: "Did you see a little girl go by?"

"No, " mumbles one after another distractedly.

And then a young man differs: "Yes!" he says. "She

was running this way," he gestures toward the busy Rue du Louvre, "—*fast*."

I address my friends who have gathered on the pavement. "I'm going this way," I say gesturing in one direction on the Rue du Louvre, "Could you go the other way?"

My friends and I disperse at a trot, the little boy forging ahead of his search squad on a scooter.

I run, frantically scanning every open courtyard and examining every darkened cross street. Nothing. This has happened too often. And there's never one time that it is less scary.

Ten eternal minutes later I hear a shout. "Luca's got her," yells the boy's mother. He found her walking around in front of the pyramid of the Louvre museum. The pyramid was nearly a kilometer from where Eurydice had started. To get there she had to cross the anarchic Rue de Rivoli, teeming as it always is with taxis and motorcycles.

We all run toward Luca, who is walking with his scooter dangling from one hand and Eurydice from the other. Eurydice looks perfectly pleased with herself.

I fall on my knees in front of the children. "Luca, thank you!" I exclaim. "Eurydice, my love. That was *terrible*. You do not go running off into the night alone! You never do that!" I say.

I hug her. I chide her. I thank my friends. I know this will happen again; I know the danger and I know the price on my nerves.

And yet I also know that stress does not only tire, it stimulates.

Dice's escapades are terrifying at the time, but the

aftermath is precious for days and months afterward in which I embrace my little runner and give thanks to the gods and to the fates for having restored her to my arms.

You get as much as you give: This is not merely a belletristic foible but a fact.

The faster I run for Eurydice, the harder I defend her to the French school authorities, the more attached to her—and inspired by her—I am.

So run Eurydice, run. I will catch you and I will love you and I will teach you and I will treasure you. Yes, I will sometimes need help; yes, I will often fear the uncertainty of it all, the total lack of guarantees—neither of proper education nor of long life—but we will be together no matter what. And I will give thanks for all I have risked for you and all that you have risked for me every day.

Chapter 16

Use What You've Got, However Slender

Eurydice being watched over by her grandparents

Having a child is not all about constant self-sacrifice. It is also about using what you've got—including what the child has got—to obtain your own ends.

As an American writer in Paris, I don't have much money, I don't have a large support system, but I do have—a handicapped pass for my daughter. So when it comes to museum visits, she goes free and so do I, as her companion. When she takes the train she goes free, and so do I. But what happens if I have the opportunity—but not the funds—to go somewhere without her?

This opportunity came up in the most macabre of contexts. A dear older friend, the journalist Alexander Cockburn, had died in California and I had managed to persuade my parents who were visiting me in France to watch Dice for the time it took me to attend his memorial service. Except that—I got the date wrong. So I had missed the memorial but still had an okay from my parents to take charge of Dice in Paris for three days as I flew to California.

Such an opportunity does not come often, so I decided to seize it. Except that instead of heading for the airport, I headed to the train station and hopped a train to Marseille. I'd never been there before and I was acutely curious about this city of sea and crime, white cliffs and dark immigrants. I also desperately needed to be alone for a few days—as everyone in an intimate, high-maintenance relationship does (and all worthwhile intimate relationships are high maintenance).

So what did I do? I booked two free tickets to Marseille—one for a handicapped child and one for her companion. Except I wasn't traveling with my handicapped child, only with her pass.

I hopped the train with a small flurry of stuffed animals and half-colored coloring books. I sat down next to Eurydice's empty seat and I started to spread them out. Train personnel came regularly, asking me for my tickets; I showed them to them, gestured to the mess next to me and claimed Dice was in the bathroom. She was visiting with a friend. She would be right back.

Three hours later I arrived in Marseille with my ghost passenger and her toys. Nobody had stopped me. My step was light as I traipsed around Marseille's beautiful old town and took up residence in a sunny private rental. I felt like a teenager again—skirting the law, rebellious in my huge Doc Martin boots, able to run, to hitchhike, to walk along the highway to the white cliffs, the Calanques, for which Marseille is known. I loved to get into seedy neighborhoods at night and drink Marseille's signature beer. It was a necessary respite.

And I'd gotten it for the worst of reasons—because of my handicapped child and my deceased friend. And yet, I did not feel guilty. Alexander, I know, would have saluted me. He knew my thoughts were with him, and if my bodily presence at his memorial was not, so be it; neither was his. As for Eurydice's pass, I felt no pang whatsoever about using it. I was doing this trip for her, in part—to keep from having single parent burn-out, to rediscover who I was when not at her side, and I'll be damned if the French rail system could not absorb the shock of a missing passenger.

I returned to Paris refreshed and light at heart, having taken pictures of graffiti and caught free rides to the beach. I embraced my Eurydice for all we were both worth. And I thanked my parents—knowing full well that what they did for a funeral they would not have done for a holiday.

When life does not put you on the top of the hierarchies of either time or money, it feels to me like you have to discover all the other hierarchies there are—from handicapped passes to convenient memorial services. The key is always to use what you've got. It may not seem like much but it is always more than we think before we delve into it. Too often self-pity blinds us to all the assets— mental and practical—that we actually have. It might be proximity to beautiful places; it might be caring friends or relatives; it might be free admission to museums or trains; it might be discounts. Our resources are like the subconscious: we only ever really use a miniature portion of them. All of our pockets are deep; we need only have the curiosity and sometimes the daring to explore them. We have little, but we also have much. Every one of us. As Emerson says, "The best of life is on the highway." Not in special collections libraries. Not in mansions or private beaches. But on the highway—available to you and me, if only we are prepared to use what we've got, to seize the opportunities that present themselves to us—all of us.

I watched Alexander Cockburn's funeral on YouTube and gave him thanks—for the triumphs of his life and for the holiday of mine.

Chapter 17

Bad Luck As Opportunity

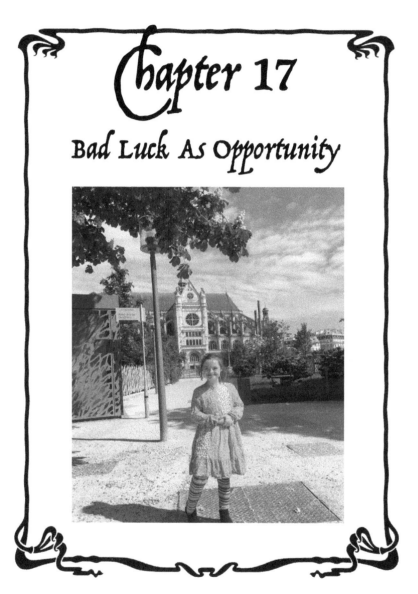

*Eurydice in our new neighborhood,
in front of Saint Eustache Church*

When I repaired to France and had submitted Eurydice's handicapped dossier, the first order of business was finding her a school for the following year. Daycare was over at three o'clock and it was pivotal to her development that we find a welcoming school. So I began what turned out to be a deeply humiliating journey.

"We don't have the structure," said the principal of a kindergarten I went to with full-blown sails of hope. Before he had heard that my child had Down syndrome, there had been lots of space and smiles all round. When I called back to ask a question about forms and to mention my child had DS, all of that changed.

Now, legally I could have forced him to admit Eurydice because French law declares, like American law, that you have a right to go to the school of your district. But the notion of forcing Eurydice into a school where the principal did not want her gave me a sick feeling in my stomach. So I continued my search. I went to a private

Catholic church up the block from me and was turned away with the same epithet (did they copy and paste from each other's dialogue?): "We don't have the structure."

At this point I was ready to move anywhere where they *had* "the structure." For while I was looking for schools I was also looking for apartments—as cheap as possible, but with a room for Dice. I was still living in a tiny studio with only curtains for partitions, like a hospital ER.

And then I heard it. In the 1st arrondissement, there was an administrator who liked children with Down syndrome. She was not the principal of a school but she was administrative head of handicapped services in a small number of arrondissements. I visited her with Eurydice. And she was smitten. "I know the school for Eurydice," she said. "It's in the 1st arrondissement. But you have to live there to get in."

Now I had never imagined living in the 1st arrondissement. With some notable exceptions (the 16th, the 6th, the 7th, the 20th arrondissements of Paris proceed in order of descending desirability)—the 1st (which contains the Louvre) being a little more desirable than the 3rd (where I lived), which is a little more desirable than the 18th or 19th. Until now I had been looking for apartments exclusively in the 3rd.

But now I had motivation for the 1st, and my apartment hunt transformed. I put my own apartment up for sale and begun to follow every lead in the 1st. There was a street I loved there—ever since the beginning of my Paris sojourns—a pedestrian market street, Rue Montorgueil, and suddenly it seemed an obvious solution. I scanned the ads and ambushed the owners, often hiding in a café across the street in order to catch them as they emerged from their buildings and to lather them in enthusiasm so they might give me prioritized consideration for the apartments I loved.

The apartment I ended up loving most—and being able to afford, with the simultaneous sale of my old apartment and the necessary help of Russell who had come into an inheritance—was a quirky place. A fifth floor walk-up, it opened into a hallway with a bathtub in it. In front of the bathtub was a window, so I could both view and be viewed in my birthday suit. But behind the quirky corridor there was a small room perfect for Eurydice as well as a larger living room. Into the main room I would build a loft bed with an office underneath—sort of a control tower from which to survey Eurydice.

For me, it was perfect. And it meant Eurydice could go to a school almost literally next to the Louvre and directly next to the Seine. A school where the principal—an ex-ballerina with inch-long eyelashes and long petticoats—loved her to pieces.

I had pitied myself so much when I was searching for schools and apartments—endless plans had fallen through—but now, through bad luck had come better luck than ever I had imagined. Never would I have dared ask Russell to advance money for a place in the 1st arrondissement—it was only through Eurydice's rejection by all the directors of lesser arrondissements, that we were forced to embrace this one.

Our nightmares become our dreams. When we are crossed in our first desires it is often that a larger—yet unadmitted—desire waits to be satisfied. If we fail to give up when things get tough, we are often surprised: The fates have bigger designs for us than we do for ourselves. So when the little things fall through, we do well to set our sights not on smaller but greater goals.

Eurydice and I now wander every day to my favorite café after school—one I went to as a foreign exchange student in Paris years ago. We have a huge sign above our fireplace which reads HOME.

Chapter 18

Dare To Be a Freak

Scattering my father's ashes

Dice and I were in Los Angeles for the winter holidays, and her grandfather was sick. Trembling on the floor sick. The night before he had still chased Dice around his patio table and drunk champagne with my mother until the wee hours of the morning. But today—the day after New Year's—he was ill. When not in bed, he lay on the couch and shook like a leaf. He had nearly a 104 fever and no amount of Tylenol or ice packages could bring it down.

Still, when Dice peered over the back of the sofa into his glazed eyes, he smiled. His brilliant, always cloud-scattering smile.

I wonder whether it's that smile that killed him. For when we took him to the Emergency Room, he wasn't taken seriously. I shouldn't even say when *we* took him to Emergency; when his house doctor—whom he had seen first—pushed him from the clinic to Emergency in a wheelchair as we followed sheepishly, even then he wasn't taken seriously. Never mind that my father—a university professor known for his erudition—could not recall the president of the country he inhabited, that he smarted from pain in his lung area which he rated as 9 on a scale of 1 to 10. Never mind that he could not hold food down, use the toilet, or even stand; that my mother and I assured the doctors we had never seen him so sick before; the smug young attending physician that day decided he had a flu. My conscientious father had had a flu shot every year long before the start of flu season. And his symptoms were far more dire than those of an ordinary flu. While he still attempted to mumble niceties to the staff and perhaps even flash his effervescent smile, he was visibly declining rapidly.

"What shall I get you from home?" I asked him. It was clear to my mother, father and me that he wasn't leaving the hospital that night. He lifted a hand dismissively. "Toothbrush?" I said, "or that bulky beige sweater of yours? A CD player? A book?"

My father, whose life was literature, frowned. "I can't understand a book now."

"Okay, no book then," I said. "Would you—"

He cut me off. "On second thought, bring me *Pinocchio*."

"*Pinocchio*?" I was taken aback. I knew my dad's tastes were peculiar at this moment but the man who taught Goethe and Nietzsche wanted—*Pinocchio*?

"To explain it to Eurydice," he said softly. Eurydice could neither speak nor read yet and was impatient even with being read to, so my father had developed the habit of pre-reading books for her and then telling her their contents in his own words while showing her the pictures.

"Okay," I said, touched. Even in his misery he was

thinking about the next day with Eurydice.

Unfortunately, there was no next day. The arrogant doctor flew past to tell us that whatever the evidence (my dad's extreme pain, high fever, flu shot, memory loss, the presence of three family members who'd had strep infections over Christmas and consumed antibiotics), my father had the flu and would benefit from "Advil and home rest."

"Don't you want to relax at home?" the doctor asked.

"No," he mumbled almost inaudibly.

"No!" my mother and I cried in unison.

"You'll be much more comfortable at home in bed," she said—and with that she instructed the nurse to pull the IVs that had been placed by her colleague for antibiotic administration and signed his discharge order. "If you feel worse, you can always come back tomorrow," she said.

It was close to midnight, and there was to be no tomorrow for my father. By 3 or 4 in the morning, he was dead.

I was at Russell's house where I had gone to retrieve Eurydice and ended up spending the night. The call came before 7. "Your father is dead," said Russell. He never minced words.

I screamed on the phone to my mother. "That's impossible! How can you know? Have you called 911?"

"That won't help anymore, that won't help anymore!" she wailed. I told her I was hanging up and calling 911. Fifteen minutes later we were all assembled at my parents' little house on Sunset Boulevard and we saw it. Death. Rigidity. Discoloration. Limbs bent in directions that were not commensurate with life. A maroon color was creeping its way up my dad's neck. His jaw was locked like steel.

"He's been dead for hours," said the paramedics. "There is nothing we can help with anymore."

What do you do when somebody dies, somebody who has in no way foreseen it and is as far as possible from "ready"? I wept. My mother was hysterical. Russell sat in my father's armchair and surveyed the decimation of the tiny Nehring family. He called the mortician. Eurydice moved from top to toe of her beloved grandfather and stroked him gently. She did not cry. She tended to him, like old wise Greek women I have seen in churches. She had the wisdom in her genes. Each of her touches seemed a blessing, a prayer.

Having my father carried out of his home on a stretcher with his face covered seemed an indignity. His face covered. Why, I thought involuntarily, he couldn't breathe that way! No matter that he no longer needed to breathe, it seemed like such a conclusive sign, an offensive sign. As though he had suddenly become a repulsive thing, the gentlemanly professor—a Halloween ghoul. I was undone.

The following days and weeks contained many things. Quietly, I set myself to writing a funeral, a funeral that opened with the *Dies Irae* of Verdi, a concert of rage rather than acceptance, by a composer my father had loved. I also talked to the LA County Coroner. We wanted to know what caused my dad's death; it would take three more months to find out, but when we did, it was obvious. He had died of strep pneumonia which rapidly turned into fatal sepsis..

My mother talked to the mortician and our relatives

in Germany. We arranged, against the opinion of the relatives, to scatter my father's ashes over the California desert he had most loved, over an old mining trail we had hiked with him countless times. And up at the top of it, Russell, my mother and I scattered the unusually heavy ashes of my father. Gravitas was what he had always had, Gravitas is what he still represented in death.

And then Eurydice and I ducked into the shadow of a boulder and opened a book. *Pinocchio*.

"He always was going to read it to you, Dicey," I said. "I'm not a literature professor like your grandfather, but let me try":

"There was an old man named Geppetto who made dolls," I began. "He made one doll, a marionette who he loved above all the rest. But he was made of wood and needed to be moved by strings. Still, he was able to talk and when he told lies—as a little boy does—his wooden nose magically grew longer and longer. Pinocchio spent all his life trying to become a flesh and blood little boy; that was his greatest wish. 'Make me a normal boy, make me a normal boy,' he would say.

"Now Pinocchio had a lot of adventures and got into some bad scrapes, but you know what? His wish was granted and he ended up being a normal boy just like he had wished, just like all the rest. But why do we read Pinocchio's story? It's not because Pinocchio ends up regular; it's because he spent so much time irregular. Pinocchio's claim to fame will never be that he was an average little boy any more than your claim to fame will be that you are an average little girl."

It's our differences that make people want to hear

about us, not our samenesses. Pinocchio's victory may have been that he turned normal—but, as Sartre said, "When you look at victory up close there is little to distinguish it from defeat." There is nothing more to say about Pinocchio once he became a regular boy. Pinocchio's tale ends when he becomes "normal." While my abnormal girl, my sweet Eurydice, is only beginning. She's different; she'll stay different; and she'll have a story to tell. A story to live. I think that is why my father's last wish was to talk with her about Pinocchio.

Chapter 19

Have The Courage Of Your Fears

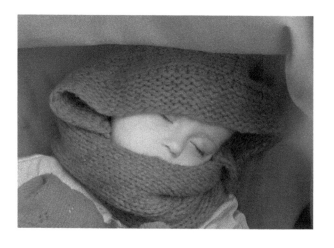

Eurydice recovering from her near-death experience

"Let me tell you something, Madame," said the man in the white coat as he flattened Eurydice's tongue with a tongue depressor. "The time you ambulanced in here with your daughter was the first—and last—time in my surgical career that I *ran* in the hospital."

I hadn't recognized him. But now the dark hair, the high cheekbones, the odd name on his lapel, Maxime Gratacap, snapped me back into a forgotten nightmare. It had been February of the previous year and I was returning to Paris from Los Angeles after the winter holidays. Eurydice and I were greeted at our flat by my friends Daniel and Smain, armed with appetizers. We all sat at my bar counter, and Eurydice began happily popping pistachio nuts while the rest of us sipped Sancerre. "Welcome home," said Daniel, "Welcome back to the land of the *aperitif*."

I was charmed. It was 11:30 at night; there was surely somewhere they needed to be—but they were here, with us.

It was good, too, to be further from the site of my father's unnecessary death after New Year's. Eurydice had pored over her beloved grandfather's dead body next to the bed where he had sunk to the floor in the night. She had stroked him tenderly while I railed in anguish at the doctors who had so underestimated his septic strep infection as to force him out of the ER hours before his death.

But as Daniel and Smain and I drank, it was Eurydice who appeared to get tipsy. Soon she was yelping for glee and laughing, and then she was choking. "No worries," said Daniel and started paddling her lightly on the back.

"Happens to all my sisters' kids," said Smain, who has nine siblings. But suddenly Eurydice was blue and her chest heaving. Daniel was rapping somewhat harder; then he was taking her by the feet and shaking her upside down.

"It'll be fine, fine," my friends murmured in unison. But all of a sudden my father's face flashed before me, and I knew things were *not always fine*. A tragedy looks like a comedy just before it happens. *Sometimes courage consists in being scared*, in listening to your fear. I had tried to articulate my fear about my sick father, but had been talked into submission.

I wouldn't let that happen again. "I'm calling emergency" I stated to Smain and Daniel and grabbed the telephone. France's innumerable disaster numbers raced through my head, 15, 12, 17, 112—I called the first and got the fire department. "You're overreacting," warned Daniel. "She just has a little something in her throat."

"She's asphyxiating," I said to the operator. The operator tried to calm me. But I'd seen enough false equanimity with my dad. "Send us someone *now*," I said.

And so they did.

As Daniel and Smain continued to chuckle sporadically at all the fuss I was making about a little pistachio,
the fire men filed up the stairs—one, two, three, four, five
of them, and hammered on the door. Even I expected that
they'd simply tip Dice over with their trained arms and
extract the offending nut, but after one look at her they
told me otherwise:

"There's nothing to be done, Madame; she goes to the
hospital or we will only make things much worse." So the
stretcher came out—my sputtering, purple child had no
idea why she was supposed to lay down—and the five
strapping young men began to rush her out the door and
down the five flights of stairs. Daniel and Smain and I had
been separated: They were to travel in a cab behind the
paramedic van while Eurydice and I traveled inside it. I
touched my cheek to Eurydice's; I had never seen her face
so full of fear.

"Calm her down," said the paramedic in the back
with me. "Nice and easy. Give her confidence." I started
to caress Eurydice's hair and strenuously radiate faith and
optimism when the message got mixed. The paramedic
at my side started to hiss at the paramedics at the front.
"Hurry up! We're losing her!" he said to the driver. "We're
losing her. Don't stop for anything on the road. She's
almost gone!"

As though I had not heard this, he turned to me and
emphatically changed his tune. "Rattle her up!" he said
"Hit her! Tickle her! Pinch her! Don't let her drift off! Don't
let her stop fighting!" Thunderstruck, I switched out my
reassuring smile for an intensive campaign of tickling,

singing out of key and screeching—anything to make Eurydice even more uncomfortable than she already was and to jog her combative instincts.

We backed into a hospital emergency section, the ambulance was opened and the heaving, tearstained, wildly staring Eurydice was rolled out. A few senseless ID conversations later and she was transferred into a nurse's station and prepared for surgery. The oxygen they were giving her wasn't getting to her and she was slowing up.

"Anguish is good!" I remember a paramedic yell at me in parting: "She has to struggle!"

"Where is the surgeon?" I asked. And then just to make absolutely sure that this was not one of those situations where hospital staff imagine that parents perhaps partially or wholly want their disabled charge taken off their hands, I started to yell, "This is a wildly adored child! This girl is loved more than anything! Don't think that because of her disability she's not wanted!" (You stop speaking subtly in these situations.) "She's the subject of books! Everybody loves her! Please, we need to save her!" It was gratuitous babble, blindly attempting to assert that this slight, averbal child was actually a VIP.

Finally a white coat came bolting down the hallway. It was Dr. Gratacap. He ran with Eurydice's stretcher-bearers to an elevator and disappeared from there to an operating room. Daniel and Smain, who had arrived in the meantime, joined me in a claustrophobic yellow corridor nearby. And we hushed.

Thirty minutes later another white coat appeared. He was the anesthesiologist. He said, "I think we are going to be able to save her." Daniel and Smain (who'd never thought anything otherwise) listened incredulously.

"Was there a chance you wouldn't?" exclaimed Smain.

"There are three separate sharp chunks of nut that have descended into her right lung. Because of the Down syndrome, she has a floppy trachea that was unable to thrust them back out. It is a dangerous situation. But the doctor has managed to photograph the pieces endoscopically, and now we are going to try to go in with endoscopic tools and take them out. This could take minutes or it could take hours. It's complicated but it doesn't look like a lost cause anymore, as it seemed when you came in."

A lost cause? We all stared. Daniel and Smain hadn't even seen minor danger. And I had only seen it, in truth, because of my father's recent, medically unanticipated death. It was his death that prompted me to abandon my habitual tough-girl stance and make a fool of myself by screaming for an ambulance over a common household incident, by crying wolf when all anyone around me saw was sheep.

Without intending as much, my seventy-four-year-old father gave his life for his granddaughter. I was sure of it, sure of Eurydice's death had my father's not predated and prevented it. The heart has its reasons that reason does not understand. As much as I feel rage at my father's death, I also thank him, as I wait in the yellow corridor, for taking Eurydice's burden onto himself.

The surgeon reemerges from the operating room and tells me it has all gone well. Eurydice is resting in the post-op room, and I can go see her. I even believe my dad—stern man that he was—would have considered his death a bargain, one that he would have accepted if asked. For in the face of Eurydice's fragility his own severity softened and blew away. He loved her ardently, this man who had never wanted to be a grandfather because it aged him. His vanity shattered like a mirror when he saw her, and his expressive face crumbled into smiles. He had become Eurydice's champion when she had leukemia. And now he had become her savior.

I talked to Eurydice a lot in the recovery room about her grandfather. Her poor neck was swollen from the passage of so many instruments, and her heart fluttered as she sobbed softly. But the air was passing freely through her two lungs, and her skin had returned to its normal hue. The surgeon came in and brought me a vial with a label. Inside were the three chunks of nut that nearly killed her. I thanked the surgeon, I thanked my dad, I thanked the gods in which I do and do not believe.

And then by chance, one year later I met Dr. Gratacap again when Dice needed her tonsils removed. And that's when he told me that this night—for him as for me—had not been like other nights. He was aware of some unusual occurrence, he said. Call it luck. Call it the courage of my fears. Call it paternal oversight. But that night, Eurydice was protected.

Chapter 20

No Man Is An Island

Yves, Eurydice and me in front of a church door in Crete

I met him at a party where Eurydice knocked over the lamp. He was there with his daughter and I was there with mine. His introduction to me was, "I need to tell you something about myself." I waited. Was he a transvestite? A serial killer? No. He was in love with his daughter as I was in love with mine. "I have an adorable little girl with all her teeth except one."

I smiled. In the past I might have cringed. As a tom-girl adolescent, I was always suspicious of men too enthralled by their children. But this time I was equally enthralled with my own child and I took the declaration as touching rather than alienating.

I looked at Jade. A boyish Eurasian, she had a whimsical smile—when she smiled—and an elfin manner. She did not smile often.

Eurydice was on the other side of the room laughing her head off over the lamp she had upset. Jade glared at her.

It was the beginning of a rollercoaster ride, the highs and lows defined by our daughters.

The first time Yves slept at my house, during his ex-partner's week with Jade, Eurydice peed on him. We had just had a night of intense platonic cuddling and we woke up to Eurydice who had climbed into my loft bed and perched herself, confidently, on top of Yves's sternum. And then, suddenly, it happened. "I'm wet," said Yves, introducing a crude note to our conversations I had not anticipated.

"Not with *desire*," he said, smiling at me with exasperation. "Your daughter peed on me!"

That's when I knew we were in this for the long haul. He was not angry. He was not squeamish. The moment did not shift to awkwardness—or animosity—as it might have. He looked at me lovingly. Eurydice dismounted and I got a washcloth with soap and slowly washed Yves's chest.

It was the start of one of the most moving love relationships of my life. But it did not last. Our daughters pulled us apart. Twenty-three and half chromosomes encountered twenty-three. The half proved critical. Radiant happiness of a seven-year-old met moody sullenness of a thirteen-year-old. Eurydice's extra chromosome seemed to be made out of love: Eurydice embraced Jade, who kept an irritated distance. It was a mismatch, pure love versus suspicious love.

I thought long and hard about loving at that stage. To love is a dangerous pursuit. I looked at Dice and I felt love swelling up in me like a rush of warm liquor in my chest and throat. I loved her to pieces, and had nearly lost her. I adored Yves, but I was not prepared to collaborate in the kind of battle he envisioned. "Our daughters are opposites" he said, as though that was a statement of the impossibility of our love. I first thought he was wrong, but he may have been right.

I asked him, a year into our relationship, if he wanted me to stay in France. Eurydice was about to switch from kindergarten to elementary school and mainstreaming is not fashionable in France. I wanted to know if he wanted me to stay no matter what—or whether if the chips fell the wrong way and Eurydice was assigned to a "medico-pedagogic facility" rather than to a mainstream school I should return to my California home and pursue less onerous options.

His answer was no answer. "You must do what is best for you," he said. Magnanimous as it was, it was not the reply I craved. I desired determination and vigor:

"We will make this work in whatever the hell country we live! As long as we are together we'll fight for our children!" It is this kind of vigor that had allowed me to keep Eurydice in excellent facilities so far.

But I got the opposite. I got flaccidness. It's not that he said, "Don't stay in Paris"—it's that he said nothing. And as little as I know about dating, I know that no answer is an answer.

I had fought like a lioness for Eurydice's French education at her many school meetings—and won. In spite of her lack of speech, twelve assembled city administrators made the considered decision to assign Eurydice to a mainstream school—of all places on the Ile Saint Louis, possibly the single most romantic spot in Paris.

When Yves told me there was a "wall" between his

daughter and me and that he could not commit to me, I knew it was the truth. Our daughters drew us in different directions. Jade's love of her father was exclusive and jealous; Eurydice's love of me was inclusive and expansive; it included all the motley crew with which I surrounded myself. I cried that night—and cried and cried. We are all absurdly fragile creatures, and without our loved ones we are lost. "No man is an island," as John Donne said.

Love is a perilous game to play—whether with a child or an adult, whether maternal or romantic. Yves threw me into a tailspin. The slightest illness of Eurydice throws me into a tailspin. People with DS used to die in the single digits. Even the DS daughter of the most famous French president, Charles de Gaulle, died of pneumonia at age 20, with all the advantages she possessed. But at the same time: love is the only game where accumulating more danger is acquiring more safety. The more you love, the more of a grip on the world you gain. The more fragile you allow yourself to be, the more other fragile persons come to your rescue. It doesn't take so very many of them.

I remember from a hospital stay how the staff rushed patients through their meals. "Don't chew, just swallow!" they would hiss at a crippled man in a wheelchair. I was surprised he could eat at all. Man is tough. But love is tougher. And if love can lead to despair, it can also lead to light, the resplendent light of a new day. The more you risk in love, the more you win.

Chapter 21

Our Strength Grows Out Of Our Fragility

Impish Dice

"**I**s it good?" the ice cream shop owner asks Eurydice, gesturing at her caramel cone.

"Giddy giddy giddy gidd*ah*!" says Eurydice. The man looks at me quizzically.

"She loves it," I say, and as though to punctuate my reply Dice takes a toothy bite out of her scoop.

Eurydice is eight years old and still does not talk. That is, she babbles vivaciously, and time and again one can make out a word in French or English or her grandmother's German, but most of the time it's babble. This in spite of her three speech therapy sessions a week; this in spite of her excellent school teacher.

But here's the thing: it doesn't matter. I take that back: it does, of course, matter for her academic progress; it matters for her recent IQ test which was abysmal. But it does not matter for her popularity in school or the joy she gives other people. It does not matter for her own happiness. At these things, Eurydice is formidable. This babbling little child takes the stage wherever she goes and gives theatrical speeches in her native jargon, reducing her audience to peals of charmed laughter. She amuses shopkeepers by knocking back her strawberry smoothie as though it was a double scotch; she hugs her classmates, and right when they start to hug her back she starts to tickle them to madness; she takes adults by the hand and domineeringly pulls them where she wants to go; she twirls her playground friends in circles until they fall from dizziness; she is invariably the most vivacious child in the park.

Is it a coincidence that Eurydice is so vivid and beloved? "Every man in his lifetime needs to thank his faults," claims Ralph Waldo Emerson. I believe that precisely because Eurydice's academic performance is so weak, her personality has become so strong; because her speech is so strange, her charisma has become so striking. Emerson points out, "Our strength grows through weakness.... A great man is always willing to be little. Whilst he sits on the cushion of advantages, he goes to sleep."

My own love of writing and reading, I believe, comes from shyness. I am perpetually at a loss of words in social settings; I am all too often at a loss for what to say and how to act. Have you "a defect of temper that unfits [you] to live in society?" asks Emerson. Are you "driven to entertain [your] self alone, and thus like the wounded oyster [you] mend yourself with a pearl?" All our pearls—my own little literary bent and Eurydice's larger-than-life personality, a blind person's superior tactile sensitivity and a deaf person's ability to read lips—are all compensations for losses or frailties. To wish away our frailties is to wish away our strengths.

I would go further and claim that if human beings are—according to some reports—the most evolved of animals, it is precisely because they are the weakest and most vulnerable animals that inhabit the globe. With no claws or fangs to fight against predators and no wings or fast legs to flee them, with no fur to protect themselves against the cold and no skin to camouflage and hide themselves, they have had to develop a host of compensatory mechanisms. Human beings, without their creations, are poor and paltry things; hairless, featherless, essentially toothless, noticeably slow and fairly unattractive bipeds. (Can you imagine a "human calendar" as opposed to a cat calendar or an exotic bird calendar? Unless one delves into pornography, the notion is preposterous.) But it is in response to all these fragilities that human beings have developed all their talents which, ultimately, have put them at an advantage over the remainder of the animal kingdom.

Even within the human race, the most sensitive tend to be the most resourceful; it is no coincidence that Napoleon was short or Proust sickly; their respective prowesses proved in large part to be results of these weaknesses.

We ought to celebrates our weaknesses like found change, discovered treasure—for they are directly redeemable for strengths and gifts.

Little wonder that Eurydice—the most vulnerable of human creatures—is also among the most buoyant; thanks, in part to her Down syndrome, she has evolved a whole repertoire of charms, of flirtation methods, of dance steps and of endearments that make the world not only her oyster but her pearl.

Chapter 22

Rejoice In What You Have, Not In What You Should Have

The first picture of Eurydice I took with the camera
Yves gave me when we separated

"*Bonne nuit, ma Precieuse*"—good night, Precious One, read Yves's nightly emails to me as I put Dice to sleep.

Yves has not stopped loving me or vice versa. We do not have a conjugal future—but I know that what he gives me is immense. The friendship, the tenderness—even the household help!—is priceless to me. When we broke up, Yves gave me the best camera I've ever had because he knows I love to take photographs and my previous camera collapsed as so many technical devices do under my care.

It is more important to me to end on loving terms than to start on them. The latter is easy; the former is far more difficult—and more rare.

I treasure my complicity with Yves, but I do not let it take over my life. Russell, too, is my right-hand man; neither of the two are typical partners. But the human spirit is wider than human relationship models. It is a mistake to think that every relationship that does not fit neatly into one of the cookie cutter forms presented to us by society is inadequate or downright insulting. Love is amorphous; love breaks boundaries; love will not dwell in cages. But above all an extra half chromosome gives an extra dose of love.

It is hard to make unconventional choices; people assume you are compromising, but the reality is that you are building larger. I won't say it's not easier to climb into the little cubby holes of marriage and cohabitation society has set out for us to occupy—I was tempted with both Yves and Russell. And those cubby holes have been offered to me by a number of men, from Eurydice's father and the gentleman in Essaouira to many others. But the truth is I am glad I declined; I am glad I was declined because my little life with Eurydice is that much more tender as a result; it is that much more privileged. Husbands are famously routinized as are their wives; lovers are attentive, impassioned and—given the right character— also astonishingly reassuring.

I would like, one day, to have an anti-marriage ceremony. Both with Yves as with Russell—a ceremony in which we pledge our love and tenderness but pledge equally not to take each other for granted, not to stuff each other into a social straitjacket.

Eurydice has few names in her vocabulary but she's got "Russell" and "Yves-oo." Just like me, she longs to be close to her favorite men—both of them. And she's not wrong.

"The heart is wider than they say," declares the narrator of a poem about a 13th century adulteress who loved her parish priest,

"It is not true
That one love casts another out
As one nail drives another nail.
Each time I love a man,
It is a shadow play, oh Father,
For the love I want to make with you.
Not pollution but a prophecy,
Not dilution but a draft.
I cannot feel a palm on my skin
Or the brush of the straw
Behind me, or a breeze
Without feeling your caress.
Every lover is you."
~Last Words of an Adulteress[1]

Every lover *is* you. It is Yves. It is Russell. And for the time being, I want very much to load my arms with their gifts rather than to send them packing. Eurydice and I are strong enough to embrace all kinds of love, all kinds of laurels. It is only myopic fixation and mindless jealousy that prevents one from reaping the abundant fruit that falls around our heads and seeps their sweetness onto our tongues.

"Russell!" says Eurydice every time she sees a man in a baseball cap or a beret. "Yves-oo!" she cries every time she sees a man with salt and pepper hair and a big smile. From the mouth of infants comes the truth—and the truth right now is that we have two opposite but precious men in our lives. May it stay that way long.

Chapter 23

Every New Beginning Is a Resurrection

Eurydice on the afternoon of New Year's Eve

It was New Year's Eve, and I was preparing to take Dice out to see friends on the Champs-Élysées. Bathed, toweled but not yet dressed, she loitered at my side, twirling her chestnut locks around her fingers and making funny faces as I applied lipstick in the mirror.

And then, without warning, she reached up and seized the crimson-colored stick and turned it into her chest.

Swush, she made a big red circle around her heart. *Swush*, she made another, smaller circle. *Swush*, there was a third circle. My porcelain-skinned girl suddenly resembled a dartboard. She colored the tiniest circle of all and she looked as if she were bleeding from a garish breast wound.

"Dice, no!" I said, wheeling to twist the lipstick from her hands.

Dice's doe eyes looked up at me, shaken. How could I be so unreasonable? She was only trying to help.

Children with Down syndrome often have extremely

acute visual and tactile memories that compensate, in part, for their limited oral and auditory memories. Dice may not reproduce many words, but she remembers gestures with preternatural precision. And she remembers that for seven months of her life nurses smeared lipstick around her chest every single day.

It wasn't actually lipstick; it was Detachol, a medical gel used to loosen bandages, but it came in a small wand, like lipstick. And day after day, medical caregivers would lay Dice back in her hospital crib, strip off her sundress and rub Detachol in concentric circles over the dressings on her chest that covered the double-lumen Hickman catheter through which chemotherapy and broad-range antibiotics, morphine and anti-fungal medications were funneled into the blood vessels nearest her heart.

This January 1 will mark the fifth year of Dice's remission. Many who thought they would survive my daughter—like my father—have preceded her to the other side. We do not know who is going to go or when.

Dice and I have our spate of issues. She has her talking problems, I have my romantic and material quandaries. But the point is not to have everything figured out; the point is to have a new lease to do the figuring. So much of what we allow to torture us, I've come to think, is self-inflicted and self-created. Why should I be sad that my girl did not sit up at so-and-so many months, or walk at a year and a half, or talk soon after? Dice listens, she laughs, she caresses; she seems extremely happy. All around us parents mutter about their kids growing up too fast. That is one problem we don't have. We are taking our bloody good time. And if Dice never talked? We would make accommodations. I have been an oddball all my life too. At least my child would have a medical explanation. We will be oddballs together.

When Dice applies lipstick to her heart today—momentarily transforming herself into a Frida Kahlo painting of a deer with a heart wound—I think she is trying to tell me something. Someone is trying to tell me how exceptionally lucky we are for this new day, for this New Year. We never know what the future holds. We are all marked; we all have our stigmata, our scars— but if we are reading this today, we are survivors. We are here because our plane did not crash, our brakes did not fail, our infection did not spread.

We like to salute beginnings, such as New Year's, but we should remember endings too. Each of us has been snatched from the jaws of death, whether we know it or not. All beginnings, in their way, are resurrections.

Chapter 23½

If You Can't Run You Were Born to Fly

Eurydice en route to Los Angeles

W e were on our way to LA for the final days of Winter break. So for the umpteenth time in Eurydice's short life, we rolled together onto a runway. But this time Eurydice looked at me with a curiosity I had not remarked before. I pulled her onto my lap and pressed her nose against the cabin window.

"There's the airport behind us," I said. "And right below us is the runway."

She looked down. Inside the plane, the flight attendants were making the safety demonstrations we knew so well. The engines started to roar to life. They grew louder and louder. I held an Evian bottle to Eurydice's lips. She ignored it. No thin libations for my daughter. She was a drinker of milk and honey, wine and wind.

"Now we're going to start rolling very fast," I explained. "We're going to go as fast as we can on the ground. We're going to race and race and try and try."

— *the plane began to rattle* —

"And when we simply can't go any faster than we're going, when we just can't do any better than we're doing on this earth,"

—*an overhead storage bin bust open*—

"then, my love, *then* we lift off into the skies."

—*I felt my seat tilt upward*—

"It's easier to fly up there than down here," I said. "It's vast. It's breezy. It's beautiful."

—*Eurydice looked at the clouds that were beginning to appear in the cabin window. She broke into a smile.*

I touched two fingers to Eurydice's rosebud mouth, and we allowed the air to bear us up.

Acknowledgments

Eurydice with Russell and her mom

This book is dedicated to its subject: *Eurydice Rafaella Tess Nehring*, my wholly unexpected little daughter and the resplendent radiance of my life.

Over the years there have been too many extraordinary doctors and nurses to thank. You know who you are, both here in Paris at L'Hopital Trousseau and Necker and in Los Angeles at the UCLA Medical Center. You saved my daughter's life–and her spirits–more than once. If I'm honest, you've saved mine, too.

I would like to thank Amelie Petit for being the first to publish my book—in her own French translation, no less.

I want to thank the 110 Press who provided a grant to Bruce Kijewksi and Michael Cohen to turn my messy English draft into a first ebook.

I want to thank Joëlle Delbourgo—my elegant, eloquent and inspired agent—for persisting in finding a home for this book in English and my charismatic, brilliant and inventive publisher, Naomi Rosenblatt, for taking it on.

I want to thank, also—in particular—Michael Bonin, my college composition teacher and—decades later—fastest friend, for teaching me how to write.

I want to thank Stephen Yenser for his marvelous mentorship and alliance throughout my Ph.D. program.

Thanks to my friends—in these pages and out—for sustaining me as I mothered, wrote, thought, struggled, and (sometimes) succeeded.

Finally, infinite thanks to Russell Jacoby, my improbable, inimitable life-love for being there for Eurydice and me—bridging large distances and age gaps—every day of the year for many, many, many years.

footnote

[1] Poem by Cristina Nehring, "Last Words of an Adulteress."

Last Words of an Adulteress

In 1274, a young woman by the name of Kate Armand was burnt at the stake in London. She was rumored to love her parish priest. Her crime was prostitution.

The heart is wider
Than they say, she said,
And stepped onto the platform.
It is not true
That one love casts another out
As one nail drives another nail.
Each time I love a man,
It is a shadow play, oh Father,
For the love I want to make with you.
Not pollution but a prophecy,
Not dilution but a draft.
I cannot feel a palm on my skin
Or the brush of the straw
Behind me, or a breeze
Without feeling your caress.
Every lover is you.
Since you cannot surround me with your touch
The wind itself must play your part
Tousling my hair and tearing at my skirts,
Raising me to your face,

And rousing my slumbering need.
Since you cannot invade me with your life
The sea itself has played your part
Rushing to fill my every pore
To gather me in its dizzy swirl,
To bear me up in white.
And since you will not grasp me in your arms
The flames themselves will lick my limbs
Must take my soul, all clean, across the continents
To your soul,
Waiting
In the smokeless still.

about the author

Cristina Nehring is a Paris-based author from California. Her first book, *A Vindication of Love*, was reviewed glowingly on the front page of the *New York Times Book Review*. She has written for the *Atlantic*, *Harper's*, *Elle*, *Oprah* and *New York Magazine* as well as for the *New York Times*, the *Los Angeles Times* and the *Wall Street Journal* and Slate, among other publications. She's nuts about her daughter.

photo©Russell Jacoby

Printed in the USA
CPSIA information can be obtained
at www.ICGtesting.com
LVHW070136261023
762122LV00007B/232